CW01190104

FERRARI

Haynes

Foulis

©Piagraph Limited and The Haynes Publishing Group 1975
First published by Ballantine Books Inc., of New York in 1971 in paperback
This hard cover edition was made in Great Britain for
The Haynes Publishing Group
Sparkford, Yeovil, Somerset BA22 7JJ
First published in hard covers September 1975
Reprinted June 1976

ISBN 0 85429 197 0

Contents

8   The slow forging of independence

12   What makes a Ferrari – and why the fuss?

34   The front engined single seaters

72   The rear engined single seaters

98   The Racing Sports Cars

136 Ferraris in the street

Photographs and illustrations for this book have been selected from the following archives: Ronald Barker, Louis Klemantaski, Montagu Motor Museum, TASO Mathieson, *Old Motor Magazine, Autocar,* Peter Garnier, Leonard Setright and Luigi Fusi, Corrado Millanta.

Ferrari

Ferrari, history of a name

People write about Ferrari, about the cars and about the man, but far too few have the opportunity or time really to know their subject. I had some of my more enjoyable times at Ferrari but also some of my most frustrating moments. Ferrari, the man or his factory, could exist only in Italy; intrigue, politics, ruthlessness, manipulation, enthusiasm, fear and a burning desire by this man to stamp his name on the pages of history, all played their part in the founding and building of the Ferrari company.

Many people have a love-hate relationship with Ferrari; love engendered by respect and admiration for what Ferrari has himself achieved in building the company.

Ferrari's main concern in this world is his name and his cars are the means by which he has imprinted that name on Italian and world history. It is sad that the age in which we live to some degree makes it difficult for characters like Ferrari to emerge; it is sad also that companies like Ferrari have to lose their identity to remain commercially viable, and must become part of larger groups such as Fiat. On the other hand I am sure that part of the success of the present cars is due to a more open outlook brought about by the involvement with Fiat, because while Ferrari was the strength for the building of his company, he was also its greatest weakness in recent years, through his unawareness with which developments were taking place and because of the many questionable advisors he gathered around him.

Yes, Ferrari is something important to all of us. Here are a man and a company interested in and in love with creating beautiful and fascinating cars. The many controversial side issues must take second place to this and I personally shall always have a very warm spot for my many friends in Maranello and for Enzo Ferrari.

John Surtees

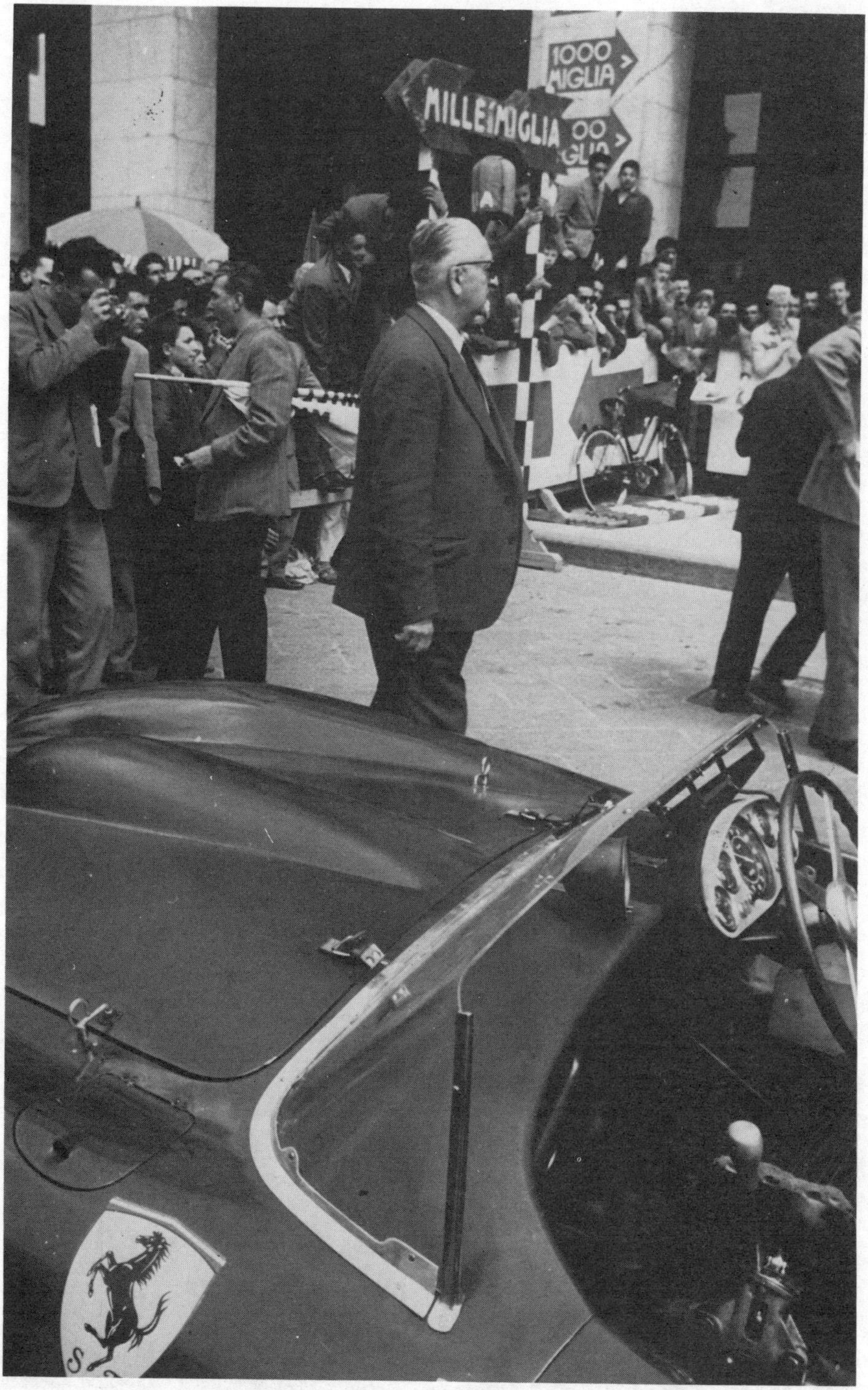
1000 MIGLIA
MILLE MIGLIA

THE SLOW FORGING OF INDEPENDENCE

Or, a horse rampant sable – this is the heraldic blazoning of the badge of Francesco Baracca, a famous Italian fighter pilot who in Spad and Nieuport biplanes was one of the leading aces of the 1914–18 war. A man in an aeroplane is as unrecognisable as a knight in full armour, but this heraldic device may have served to inform at least some of his thirty-five defeated adversaries that they had been shot down by no less an opponent than Francesco Baracca. Then one day in 1918 it was Baracca's turn to be sent down. That badge, painted on a piece of his aeroplane's fabric, was recovered and sent to his parents, and they kept it until one day in June 1923 when it seemed to them that there was another young Italian whose skill and courage fitted him to bear that same shield.

The young man was Enzo Ferrari, who had that day driven an Alfa Romeo in a race at Ravenna with such virtuosity as to overcome much more powerful opposition, to win the race and establish a lap record, to set the crowd wild with applause and enthusiasm. He was twenty-five years old.

Of his courage and audacity there can be no doubt. Morally and commercially he exercises them to this day. Enzo Ferrari is physically a big man, temperamentally and historically a great man. He has borne that badge, the *cavallino rampante,* on the racing cars he drove, then on those of the Scuderia Ferrari team of racing Alfa Romeos in the 1930s, and finally set it on the long and justly renowned series of cars that have issued from his own factory.

He was born on 18th February 1898 in a house on the outskirts of Modena. His origins have been described as middle-class by American writers, as humble by English; but the facts are that his father was a metal worker who built axles and roofs for the Italian railways, a man whose station in life was such that he was one of the first in Modena to own one of the new motor cars. Young Enzo found this a most intriguing apparatus, and his enthusiasm was fanned by visits to motor races, his first being made at the age of ten years. By the time he was thirteen he was learning to drive, and he pursued his enthusiasm for the petrol engine in assisting his father, whose business had diversified to include motor repair work. In the army during the First World War he worked as a motor mechanic, and when he was demobilised he tried to get a job with Fiat. His father and brother had died during the war and Enzo himself was invalided out of the army with nothing much more than a letter of introduction to Fiat from his colonel. He had a little money, but in the absence of a job, either with Fiat or with anyone else, the necessity of living soon consumed it. At last he found employment as test driver for a little firm which converted light Lancia trucks into passenger cars, and he came to know more and more of the people who figured in the post-war car boom, many of whose names are now legendary. He also learned a great deal about advanced driving techniques when he went to work for a small motor manufacturer, CMN. Eventually, after some importuning by the young man, they entered him to drive in a hill climb, in which he finished fourth, and this encouraged them to enter him in the Targa Florio.

At last Ferrari was beginning to make an impression on the curiously closed world that he sought to join, and in 1920 he entered the service of Alfa Romeo driving their cars in competition, starting with the 1920 Targa Florio in which he finished second. Throughout the rest of the decade Ferrari's reputation as a driver grew and grew, and so did the competition activities of Alfa Romeo, until the point was reached in 1929 when they had to hand over the responsibility of racing their cars to some organisation that could function outside the factory. The man they chose to command it was Enzo Ferrari, and he took over all their racing equipment and some of their technicians, installing them in a new two-storey building

Enzo Ferrari

where the racing cars of Scuderia Ferrari were prepared alongside the cars that the factory sold to private owners.

In his new position Ferrari was no longer driving. Instead he devoted himself to administration, for which he revealed surprising ability. It was administration of a very autocratic kind, for Ferrari could brook no indiscipline. The drivers that he engaged were invariably the finest available, including such notabilities as Campari, Nuvolari and Varzi. So long as they did as they were told and won their races, Ferrari and Alfa Romeo were happy; but as the years passed, the wins became less frequent. The new formula which came into effect in 1934 embodied regulations which were exploited to the utmost by the Auto-Union and Mercedes-Benz teams, which suddenly blossomed with National Socialist Germany to dominate motor racing with cars of such advanced design and power as had never been seen before. The Alfa Romeos, badly outdated and outpaced, had eventually to be withdrawn; and in 1938 Alfa Romeo shifted their attention from Grands Prix to the races for 1½-litre voiturettes.

It was not to be Scuderia Ferrari that would race the new Alfa but a new factory organisation, Alfa Corse. But they found work there for Ferrari, where he collaborated with Gioacchino Colombo in the design of the new car, the type 158. For a year or so Ferrari stayed on, but his independent spirit could not endure the overriding authority of the Spaniard Wilfredo Ricart who had been appointed director of the racing division, and the two men fought bitterly. In the circumstances it had to be Ferrari who left. A man less sternly independent, less intolerant, less courageous could never have got that far – nor have gone on, as Enzo Ferrari did, to become one of the greatest individuals in the history of the motor car, a manufacturer whose reputation ranks with that of Birkigt, Bugatti, Roesch and Royce as one who has made major and lasting contributions to the development of character, capability and nobility in the motor car.

All those other great men have long passed away, but Ferrari remains the significant figure in the racing scene that he has been for practically half a century.

His cars have seldom been remarkable in their specifications. He has always been content for others to do the pioneering, preferring the natural role of a classicist. In Grands Prix, Ferrari

Young Enzo posed at the wheel of a P2 Alfa Romeo, one of the cars of the Scuderia Ferrari which he ran

was the last serious entrant of a front-engined car, the last champion of the six-cylinder engine, the last to field a car running on wire-spoked wheels. Even when his racing fortunes have been at a low ebb, his name has commanded respect in any entry list. His cars have six times carried the world's champion driver, in 1952, 1953, 1956, 1958, 1961 and 1964. In the fifteen years during which he maintained an unbroken record of participation in the long-distance classics counting towards the sports car manufacturers' championship, Ferrari won it ten times. Ferrari may not be unconquerable, but he is perennially irrepressible.

WHAT MAKES A FERRARI – AND WHY THE FUSS?

The race for the Coppa Franco Mazzotti, vulgarly known as the Mille Miglia, was run over a closed circuit in 1940. It may seem remarkable that it was run at all, for the times were hardly conducive to the proper organisation of any kind of international sport. Indeed it was a somewhat unreal Mille Miglia, conducted over a relatively short route around Brescia rather than over the classical figure of eight that stretches down to Rome and back. It must have seemed particularly unreal to the German participants, permitted and even encouraged by a propaganda-conscious state to engage in sporting combat at a time when most of their compatriots were committed to a bloodier kind of fight.

Drinking with the German drivers at the cafés around the circuit during the practice days before the race, that great Italian driver Count Lurani made a point of wearing his racing overalls, emblazoned with the badge of the British Racing Drivers' Club whose prominent Union Jack must have caused the Germans some embarrassment. When the race came, they had their revenge: it was the Germans who dominated it with their exceptionally fast BMW 328 cars, the winner being a special-bodied version in the hands of Baron von Hanstein, subsequently to earn world-wide respect and affection as the racing director of Porsche.

But to Italians in that still peaceful 1940, before the fateful 10th June when Mussolini plunged them into war, the most notable personal touch to the race was the reappearance of the name of Ascari, a revered name associated with great achievements in the far-off Alfa Romeo days before the great Antonio Ascari met his tragic death in the French Grand Prix at Montlhéry in 1925. Now here was the son Alberto Ascari, destined to become world champion after the war but at this stage making his debut in serious racing. To an Italian with a feeling for the continuity of a great tradition, Ascari's was not the only debut, though he was strongly associated with the other. For on the list of entries could be read against No 66 *Concorrente, Scuderia Ferrari; Vettura, Ferrari 815; Conduttore, Alberto Ascari*.

He was not alone in the car, being partnered by Giovanni Minozzi. Nor was theirs the only car, for No 65 was driven by the Marquis Rangoni, partnered by Enrico Nardi.

During the first lap of the triangular course between Brescia, Cremona and Mantua the fifteen cars in the 1.5-litre class were led by Ascari; but a valve spring broke and Ascari's lead was taken up by Rangoni, who held it until the last lap when a timing chain broke while the car had a thirty-three minute lead over its nearest competitor.

Rangoni was killed during the war. The car he drove still exists in Italy, in a private collection. It has often been reported that the type 815 Ferrari was based on the cylinder blocks of two Fiat 1100 engines, but in fact it was the cylinder heads of the type 508C Fiat that were strung out in line ahead beneath that broad Ferrari bonnet. The straight-eight cylinder block was an aluminium casting built specially for Ferrari in Bologna, as were the valve gear cover and the sump. Ferrari himself made the cast iron cylinder barrels and a steel crankshaft whose five main bearings were of standard Fiat dimensions. There was good reason for this free use of Fiat components: not only were they sturdy and freely available, but Fiat were offering substantial awards for class victories by cars admitting to a substantial Fiat basis. For all his other outstanding attributes, Ferrari would not have got where he is today were he not also a shrewd business man, and the availability of such bonuses presumably influenced him in his use of connecting rods, valves, valve springs and rocker arms of Fiat manufacture.

It may have been these components of humble origin that limited the Ferrari engine to 5500rpm, despite the minute

Bracco in the 1949 Mille Miglia with a Type 166, in which Maglioli accompanies him as co-driver

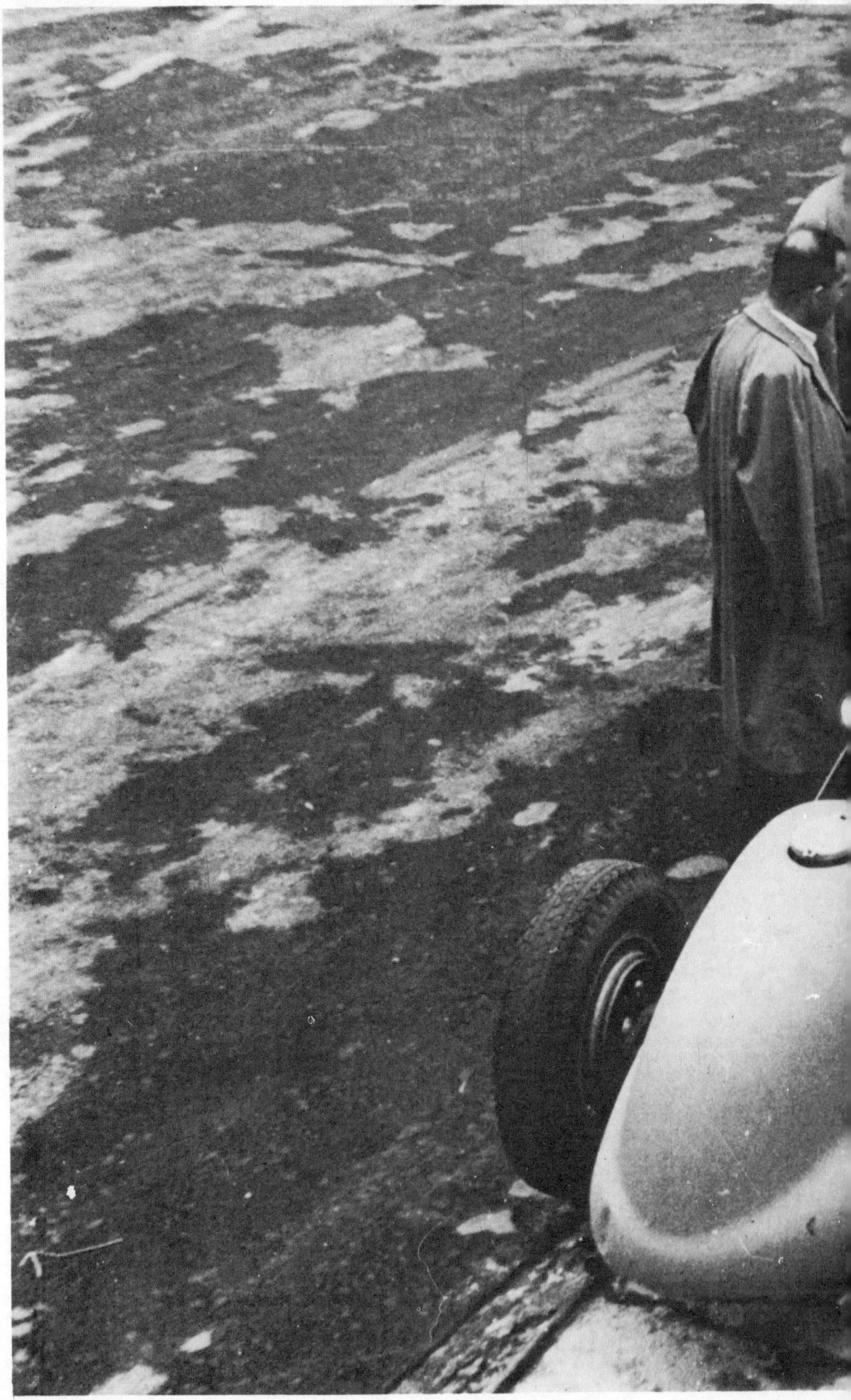

Conference during testing of the 1940 F2 prototype. At the extreme right of the group is Lampredi

Above: The two first Ferrari cars, the AAC 815 two seaters, in the 1940 Mille Miglia. Leading is number 66, Ascari. Below: The winner of the 1949 Mille Miglia, Clemente Biondetti, in his Type 166 Touring Barchetta Ferrari. This was his fourth victory in the race: in 1938 and 1947 he won for Alfa Romeo, in 1948 and 1949 for Ferrari. Below right: A very early Type 125 sports-racing Ferrari. Wearing glasses is the distinguished British writer, the late L E Pomeroy

cylinders whose bore of 63 millimetres was complemented by a stroke of a mere 60 – a stroke : bore ratio which, being less than unity, represented a marked departure from accepted dogma and set the pattern for all future Ferrari engines. Whether it was in fact the valve gear or perhaps the manifolding (though four Weber carburettors were a generous allotment by the standards of the time) the engine developed only 72bhp at 5500rpm. However, the car weighed only 635 kg complete, and could reach 165kmh, and there seems no doubt but that the 22-year-old Ascari made the most of it.

It may have been a deliberate mistake that the entry list described the car as a Ferrari 815. The name Ferrari was not supposed to be featured: according to his contract of severance with Alfa Romeo, Ferrari was not to build or race a car under his own name for four years. Still smarting from the circumstances of his disagreement with Ricart which had led to his leaving Alfa Romeo, Ferrari had gone off to Modena with Luigi Bazzi, Alberto Massimino and others, and set up a firm bearing the innocuous title Auto Avio Costruzioni.

It was presumably more than coincidence that the personnel constituted a splendid basis for a racing organisation; and when a couple of customers begged Ferrari to build some cars suitable for the forthcoming Mille Miglia, he rose to the occasion. The decision to build the car was taken on Christmas Eve 1939, and the design of it was entrusted to Massimino. Nardi, then on Ferrari's staff and after the war a well-known specialist car manufacturer in his own right, did the testing and helped in the development. It was very much a rush job, and such limited results as it achieved did credit to those who were concerned with it. Ferrari directed operations, and the mechanical failures which eliminated the cars from the race certainly did not disgrace anybody concerned; but it was the last we were to hear of Ferrari

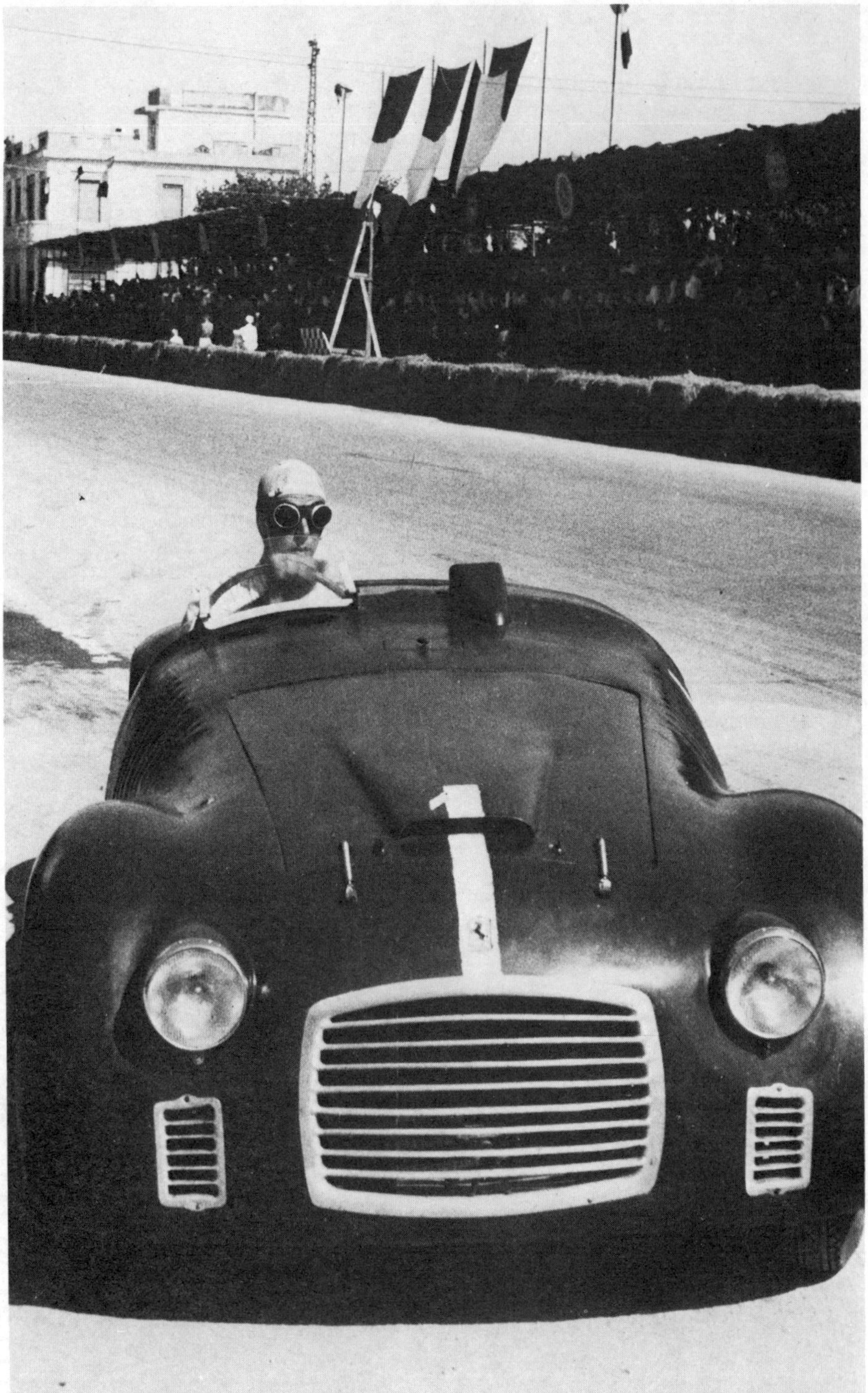

for several years. He spent the war running his business as a machine tool specialist, his works being moved by the government in 1943 from Modena to a site at Maranello, quite near where the present Ferrari factory is to be found.

It was a period when even the closest knit organisation could expect ruptures and dismemberment: the Ferrari factory was bombed in November 1944 and again in February 1945, but somehow Ferrari was ready to resume racing after the war. As for personalities, the Spaniard Ricart was forced by Fascist pressure to quit Alfa Romeo in 1940 and made no further impact on automobile history until he emerged as the designer of the brilliant, expensive and undeservedly unsuccessful Pegaso, built by ENASA in the old Hispano-Suiza works at Barcelona. This appeared in 1951 and in concept was everything that the Ferrari could have been. But it was not a success, being more the victim of circumstances than of any innate failing; whereas, of course, by that time Ferrari was a name that inspired respect, and within a few years his cars were to be of comparable merit. It is interesting but hardly rewarding to speculate on the possible consequences had Ricart remained with Alfa Romeo.

As it turned out, it was somebody else from Alfa Romeo who joined Ferrari as chief designer of the first post-war car to bear his name. This was Colombo, with whom it will be remembered Ferrari collaborated in the design of the type 158 Alfa Romeo racing voiturette. Ferrari meant to go racing seriously, and he must have known what he would be up against, at least from Alfa Romeo; and so must Colombo, who set himself to design a 1½-litre car which might form the basis not only of a commercially viable sports car but also of one that might participate effectively in Grands Prix run under the new 1½-litres super-

Cortese in a Type 166 at Pescara for the 1948 race

charged or 4½-litres unsupercharged formula.

There is no doubt but that Colombo was a gifted designer. The ineffable superiority of his type 158 Alfa Romeo throughout the late 1940s, while Ferrari struggled to become competitive, may be sufficient evidence in itself; but when, disenchanted with the work of this great man, Ferrari sent him packing and transferred the responsibility to Lampredi, Colombo went to Maserati and wrought wonders there. He began with the 2-litre A6G (upon which a lot of work had already been done by none other than Massimino) and culminated his work with the type 250F Grand Prix car which appeared in 1954, and gave Ferrari increasingly strong opposition in Grand Prix racing throughout the following four years. Then, as if to prove as with Ricart that engineering merit is not alone sufficient, he went to Bugatti and devised the very unconventional type 251 which ran in the 1956 French Grand Prix. It was dismissed as an abject failure and was never seen again, despite its embodiment of features that in retrospect can be seen to have been far ahead of their time.

In the meantime Ferrari had the relatively unproven Aurelio Lampredi as a source of engineering inspiration. He was not as completely unproven and unqualified as some commentators have suggested, having been responsible for the very sophisticated rear-engined V8 Isotta Fraschini saloon prototype, whose failure to go into production was no fault of his. The chronicle of Lampredi's work for Ferrari will be told later, as will that of Colombo and others; but the point that must be made here is that Ferrari soon showed himself in those early post-war years to be utterly ruthless in his hiring and firing. If you are going to be a bear, you might as well be a grizzly bear; if you are going to be an autocrat, you must brook no arguments. Time and again, Ferrari's response to failure or dissension has been dismissal: first Colombo, then Lampredi and later

Above: The type 166 F2 engine of 1950. Six studs in line along the camshaft cover shows this to be a Colombo design; there are seven on a Lampredi engine. Below: By 1958 the competition V12 had advanced to this, the 3-litre Testa Rossa

Chiti among the most noteworthy of his engineers. Behra and Surtees are among the drivers who have successively clashed and departed, while the merciless and intolerant old martinet stayed on ruling the roost.

It is not surprising in these circumstances that the kaleidoscopic changes of Ferrari's fortunes in racing during the first two post-war decades were counterpointed by an equally ill regulated series of roadgoing production cars of variable quality and appeal. Little spiky cars, big hairy ones and one or two distinctly woolly ones bore the prancing horse emblem over the roads of Europe and even across the seas to America, earning for their constructor a vast amount of money and a somewhat ambivalent reputation.

As is usually the case, the first ten years were the worst. Already a great name, Ferrari did not then have the stature or the resources to undertake the manufacture of all, or even of the majority, of the cars' components. Axles, gearboxes and other parts would come from improbable and not entirely suitable sources such as the thoroughly humdrum Fiat 1400 saloon, and if such components failed to survive the treatment meted out to them it was certainly not Fiat's fault. Furthermore, Ferrari's preoccupation with engines left his cars seeming sometimes distinctly primitive in comparison with those of certain rivals which never made such a gorgeous noise but which would go reasonably well and steer and stop a good deal better. The popular story of the mechanic in the tool roll gave a clue to the unreliability and quirkiness of the early production Ferraris, a reputation that was fairly deserved. The cars should also have had a reputation for being noisy, rough-riding, heavy to handle, temperamental, vibratory and often deficient in braking ability. The fact that they did not may be due in part to the understandable reluctance of the owner of an expensive and unusual car to admit his error of judgment in buying it; and in part to the rarity of these cars which meant that a few were scattered over a wide area. The factory propagandists, the press and other adulators were always loud in admiration and wonder, while the critic was often a voice in the wilderness.

Things improved somewhat in the late 1950s, so that the 250 GT series and its successors in the first half of the following decade were much more completely engineered and more generally satisfactory. Design faults were no longer the results of inadequate resources but the unpardonable consequences of careless and superficial direction. The best example is the notorious case of the Laycock de Normanville overdrive which was hung as an appendage behind the four-speed gearbox of certain cars in the 250 GT series: the gearbox had to be lubricated with a certain type of oil, the overdrive could only function and survive when charged with oil of a different type – but the oil pumped through the overdrive had to come from and return to the gearbox! It was such a situation as Dorothy Parker might best summarise: *with this the gist and sum of it, what earthly good can come of it?*

Most failings were less serious than this, though at Ferrari prices, bearing in mind the purchase price, the cost of spares, and the rapacity of Ferrari agents in some quarters, the smallest peccadillo may become expensive. But it would be wrong to suppose that Ferrari in those days was aiming to cater for the Rolls-Royce market, for his preoccupation with racing was as complete as ever and it was sufficient for his purposes if he sold enough street Ferraris of sporting temperament to finance his racing operation.

One must also consider the typical customer and what he sought and expected to find in his Ferrari. As like as not the car was to him a mere plaything, an indulgence, a cosmetic. Look at some of the special bodies created on early Ferraris and you are forced to doubt the seriousness of the owner's intention. Probably the thing would be

The Ferrari factory during construction of cars for the 1955 Mille Miglia. Number 705 is Maglioli's 118 LM

The Ferrari factory in 1960, with 250GT production in full swing. Note the chassis frames

The Pininfarina 250GT, in the version introduced in 1959, on the assembly line

driven gently on most of its outings, the proprietor revelling in the selfish luxury of a silky smooth power plant that seemed inimitable and heralded itself and him with a gorgeous garrulous whoop of exhaust and scream of machinery that was almost indescribable and never less than exciting. Such idiosyncrasies as a fragile clutch, a dubious final drive, recalcitrant electrics, water pumps that leaked into the sump, and a turning circle that might pass muster on a Greyhound bus might pass unnoticed. The ride was hard, but it was not necessarily a fault. Other cars were murderous to the stomach, the Ferrari directed its attack to the kidneys. It was neither better nor worse, but merely different.

When the 250 series expanded itself by a litre to become the 330, the character of the car changed somewhat. There was now a wider spread of torque, a greater sense of bulk, more evidence of the ascension of roadholding over handling, and a growing awareness of the need for power steering. On the other hand there was no sign of any more appreciation of the need for good finish and high standards of construction in the body: water could get in almost anywhere, carpets and trim were of dubious quality and ephemeral life, while door and window fittings and heater arrangements often seemed inadequate or even shoddy. No longer just so much fire and brimstone in a lashed-up package, the Ferrari was not yet a sporting carriage in which a gentleman might go anywhere, but rather something for a spiv to drive in a kindly climate.

By this time, about the mid-1960s, the Ferrari organisation had become much more soundly established and could set about car manufacture in a much more thorough and professional way. It did not in the process lose that special romantic aura which attaches to the car makers of Modena and cannot be discerned in any country outside Italy. This is partly due to the presence of the autodrome in the town where a great deal of serious testing is done. It is also done at Monza and on the singularly convenient Autostrada del Sole, where Ferraris, Maseratis and Lamborghinis meet for a lot of testing and not a little unofficial competition. The people in the locality have grown used to the idea of highly tuned multi-cylindered projectiles issuing from one or other of these three factories and haring off up the road, dodging the bicycles and bullock carts and Fiat 500s on the way to a workout in the mountains or on the motorway. Particularly in the case of Ferrari, it is as likely to be a hyper-sports machine as a grand tourer, though they are all driven in much the same way and the principal difference is in the amount of noise and the width of the black lines left on the road by spinning rear wheels outside the factory gates.

Inside those gates, the Ferrari organisation functions as a sort of cross between an art studio and a laboratory. The engineering work is of a very high calibre, but it does not obscure the traditional Italian view of a fine motor-car as an artefact to be worked on with all the craft and sympathy that make efficiency and beauty interdependent, in the tradition established by a long line of genius dating back to the Renaissance. It is a wealthy organisation and was so even before it was taken over by Fiat, for the Torinese concern injected large but undisclosed annual sums every year, recognising that the glory of Ferrari did a lot of good for the reputation of the country in general and the Italian motor industry in particular. With this aid, and thanks also to the inspired commercial management which is directly responsible to Ferrari himself, there is enough money available to ensure that whatever is done should be done well.

It is a compact factory, employing perhaps 500 people, but the important thing about them is not their number but their qualities. A remarkably high proportion of them are craftsmen and engineers of the highest calibre, for Ferrari has for years made a practice of skimming the cream of the technical high schools and universities. This perfectionist attitude is reflected in the work of every man, designer and builder alike, with the utmost care being taken in the assembly and con-

An extremely popular version of the 250GT was this 2+2 by Pininfarina

struction of the cars. A lot of the work is done by hand, and where machinery is preferred it is always the finest and most highly developed of its kind. The result is a product that is produced to a standard that is matched by few other constructors. Indeed, so far as the mechanical components of the car are concerned, it is safe to say that only Rolls-Royce, Bristol and Lamborghini reach the same standards. It is probably not irrelevant that they are about as expensive as a Ferrari. Machining tolerances are close. Every finished part is subjected to non-destructive testing, such as crack testing, radiography, or whatever might be appropriate, and there is a rigorous tracing of flaws to their source.

This can be done because Ferrari try to make as much of their cars themselves as they possibly can. The degree to which they succeed is quite extraordinary considering how small their production is. A particular point to note is that the factory has its own foundry where all necessary castings are produced, including those in some of the more difficult alloys. It was not always so: ten years earlier, cylinder heads and blocks were produced for Ferrari by Maserati. But now there is an extreme reluctance to entrust any work to anybody else. Plating, heat treatment, and virtually everything except electrics, hydraulics and bodywork are done on the premises in the knowledge that if there is nobody else to blame there is also nobody else to suspect.

Bodywork has never been a Ferrari forte, although the shells of some of the newer competition cars are made on the premises. Apart from these few exceptions, standard Ferrari bodies are designed by Pininfarina, and the majority of them are built by that firm in their big factory on the outskirts of Turin. Chassis are taken there bare and come back clothed for insertion of mechanical components on a slowly moving assembly line. The more sporting Berlinetta bodies, although of Pininfarina design, are built by Scaglietti, who are nearby in Modena. But the working principles are the same.

It may be because of this tendency to dissociate themselves from bodybuilding that Ferrari can devote such especial pains to the manufacture, assembly and testing of their engines. About 70 man-hours go into the assembly of a standard V12 to very precise tolerances, after which the engine is run in on the bench for ten hours in a cycle that varies the speed between 1400 and 3600 rpm. The next two hours are spent between 4000 and 6000, after which a power output check is made. If everything is satisfactory the engine can then be installed in a car which, when completed, will be taken out for a test run of half an hour's duration.

During 1970 the factory was extended by the erection of a special new wing devoted to the manufacture of the Fiat Dino, whose engine is derived directly from the eponymous Ferrari V6. This is one of the visible signs of the collaboration which has long existed between Fiat and Ferrari, and which came into the open in 1969 when the former officially and financially embraced the latter, making the Fiat Dino a rare automotive example of legitimation *per matrimonium subsequens*.

It is more than likely that this association with Fiat has had something to do with the comparatively unruffled atmosphere which prevails at high level in the Ferrari design staff nowadays. The days of acrimony and high speed firing seem to have passed: Ing Rocchi has master-minded Ferrari engine design since the late 1950s and Michael Parkes has been chief development engineer during the mid-sixties. It is impossible to over-estimate the contribution made by these two men to the perfection of the modern Ferrari, and therefore to the fortunes of the firm. It was Rocchi who put Ferrari back on the racing map with the V6 engine when the old Colombo based V12 and the Jano and Lampredi versions of the V8 had become obsolete. It was Rocchi again who more recently evolved a new line of 12-cylinder engines to do battle with the unholy rabble of English and American V8s that have corrupted racing in the latter 1960s. As for Parkes, formerly an architect of the exquisite and underrated little Hillman Imp and son of that most gentlemanly chairman of Alvis, it is probably he more than anyone who is responsible for the considerable elevation of quality standards in production Ferraris.

This work has not involved merely the setting of standards and where those standards might be acquired; but goes beyond this to a revision of the order of priorities in the evolution and production of a car that is to be offered for sale to the public. It involves in the first place an analysis of the customer's psychology: for an Italian customer is totally different from an English one, and standards expected by the one are very different from those accepted by the other. Parkes admits to having bent the compromise towards a motor car that would suit the British type of customer and the Italian – and by inference all those intermediates who cannot be aligned with one extreme or the other. Nevertheless he, just like everybody else on the staff, was always aware that the car is called a Ferrari, and that Ferrari is the man who makes the decisions. It is Ferrari who decides the specification of the car he wants, and although he is not involved in the detailed design, he is very much responsible for the basic rightness of that car. It was the task of Parkes and his colleagues to ensure that what is designed is consonant with Ferrari's expressed intention. Parkes therefore spent a lot of time in the drawing office, despite an obvious predilection for racing. His exploits on the track reached a peak in 1966 and '67, only to be brought to a lengthy halt by a serious accident in the 1967 Belgian Grand Prix.

All his engineering skill and racing experience were called upon as he contributed to and criticised the developing design. If he felt strongly about something he had to be there when Ferrari came by so that he could make his point about the need to conform with legal requirements in this country or satisfy the practical requirements imposed by topographical or social phenomena in that country. Dusty roads in South Africa, repeated hill starts in San Francisco, freezing fog over the Pennines or tropical heat in Queensland, all have to be taken into account. In effect Parkes had to make the Ferrari a more usable car in general circumstances, as opposed to its earlier particular set of circumstances in which it shone.

In fact the earlier context for a Ferrari car was Ferrari's own driving experience and even his individual driving technique. For example, if there was a traffic jam he would park his car outside a café and go inside; when the traffic had gone he would get in the car and go again – and that means of course he did not find out a lot of the things that happen in traffic.

This enthusiasm for the actual business of driving is general among the Ferrari staff (it is difficult to imagine anyone being there who did not feel that way about driving) and it tends to give them an unbalanced order of priorities, reflected in the somewhat lopsided character of the cars themselves. When Parkes first went to Ferrari he found that one of his problems lay in restraining people's enthusiasm and inventiveness rather than encouraging it, for they were generally happier to conceive the next racer than to nurture the last tourer. As a result, such items as heating and ventilating systems were still rather primitive and inadequate, and body finish was poor. This was a real problem, for Ferrari do not make the bodies themselves. Yet to the average customer the fixtures and fittings of the car seem more immediate and important than the engine, despite the fact that it is the engine more than anything else that has given the Ferrari its reputation and attracted the customer in the first place.

It seems to be an unfortunate fact that many customers simply do not appreciate the niceties of the twelve-cylinder

Michael Parkes

engine. As many as 80 or even 90 per cent, according to Mr Parkes' estimate, fail to see how beautiful a car is mechanically, preferring to judge it by how the doors open and close and whether the water gets in and whether the heater blows hot or cold. In these and many other things Ferrari are in the hands of their body builders. Scaglietti are not difficult, being in Modena and very much under Ferrari control. It is easy for someone to go down the road to their works and indulge in a little shouting and table-thumping. By these means and doubtless by others more subtle, Ferrari get good results from Scaglietti — but Scaglietti, being limited to the production of the GT Berlinettas, do not make many cars. All other standard bodies are turned out by Pininfarina in Turin, which is considerably more distant.

And this is only part of the problem. A major difficulty is that production is in low quantities. This means it is often impossible to justify special tooling: for instance it is not admissible to make a mould for a special rubber section to seal the quarter lights, so Ferrari have to do as best they can. The outcome is not as good as on a much cheaper car made in far greater numbers, where it is economically feasible to tool up in a big way for such small details. It is in body items of such a small nature that Ferrari still suffer most, either because they have to take proprietary parts which come from another car (door locks and window locks for example) or else make every one by hand, which is expensive, time-consuming and sometimes impossible anyway. It is not altogether fair to blame Pininfarina for these short-comings. The coachbuilder is very conscious of the difficulties, but he is after all a businessman and cannot extend philanthropy to the subsidising of Ferrari in such unprofitable details. Other manufacturers whose cars are clad by Pininfarina include Alfa Romeo, Fiat and Peugeot — all firms which turn out cars in very large numbers, and are able to afford the cost of a resident inspector at the body factory. For Ferrari to do the same would not make sense, for an inspector working in Turin can hardly justify his employment by inspecting two or three cars a day.

It would of course be folly to dampen the enthusiasm of Ferrari designers and workers for their magnificent engines, since in the final analysis it is the engine which is the be-all and end-all of any Ferrari. Nobody can make the perfect motor car, and it is up to each manufacturer to determine his own form of compromise and arrive at his own particular approach to perfection. Every car may be perfect in one respect: the Lotus in steering, the Citroen in ride control, the Rolls-Royce in its coachwork. In Britain, where a Ferrari costs about the same amount of money as a Rolls Royce, there is a strong tendency among customers to judge the Ferrari by the same standards of superficial finish. This is a mistake, unless the customer really wants a Rolls-Royce, because in a Ferrari a higher proportion of the purchase price has been devoted to making the engine mechanically perfect.

This brings us back to the fact that it is Ferrari himself who establishes the basic specification of each new model. He must be recognised as an old stager, brought up in an age when the engine was all-important and the chassis and suspension were matters for the blacksmith. Could his conceptual concern explain the emphasis on engines, transmissions and external shape and the disregard, until relatively recently, for the finer points of structural design? He has never seemed to pay much attention to the chassis of the Ferrari: it is difficult to see where it is, for the shape of the car does not seem to be determined by the chassis. If you burrow down far enough you find a sort of multi-tubular platform so shallow as to prompt doubt about its beam or torsional stiffness. It is not just that Ferrari is still tempted to live in the days when the chassis was a flexible thing. It is as much a question of local conditions and convenience dictating the design and inhibiting the choice of something more sophisticated. Most Ferrari chassis are welded tubular structures so it is very easy to start making one with the minimum of tooling, and also to change it if a modification or improvement should be indicated. If expensive tooling were specified for pressing out side members or backbone centre sections then it would have to be justified by a long production run; and this is something which is quite foreign to the nature of Ferrari production. Quantities are usually very low indeed and it is unusual for more than three or four hundred of any one particular model to be built in a year. If Ferrari made more cars, and yet not enough to match the best and most self-sufficient of mass producers such as Ford, they would be forced to farm out much more of their work and be less self-contained, less able to make everything themselves to ensure that it is made the way they want it.

It is of course arguable that in some cases the specialist component supplier can do a bettter job than the all-round manufacturer, and do it more cheaply. Take crankshafts for example: if Ferraris were being made in larger quantities, large enough to justify sub-contracting such work, the crankshafts might be produced more cheaply than Ferrari can do it, and might not need to be machined all over as is the impressive six-throw seven-main-bearing crankshaft of a V12 Ferrari engine. It sounds very romantic and the essence of perfectionism for Ferrari to turn each crankshaft out of a solid steel billet; but it is not necessarily the best way to do it, not necessarily good engineering at all. A forged crankshaft, whose skin is machined as little as possible, may be blessed with a far more beneficial grain flow within the metal, making the crankshaft actually stronger and more durable than the individually machined examples that find their way into Ferrari engines.

Yet, as it happens, the Ferrari crankshaft has to be machined all over in any case because the clearances in the block are so small that a raw forging could not be tolerated. Besides a twelve-cylinder crankshaft with seven main bearings is an extremely difficult thing to forge at all because of its complexity. The dies would be enormously expensive, and even when the forging process was finished the shaft would still have to be put into a machine and finish-cut all over. If this must be done, why not start by machining a bar in the first place? It may be idle to point to the distinguished diesel engine manufacturers such as Maybach and Bristol Siddeley whose forged V12 crankshafts are machined all over, for these are very big and questions of scale are important in the application of forging techniques. More recently, methods have been developed for forging crankshafts with 120-degree throws (appropriate to the shaft of a three, six or twelve-cylinder engine) by forging the shaft initially as a single-plane affair with throws set at 180 degrees, after which the shaft may be

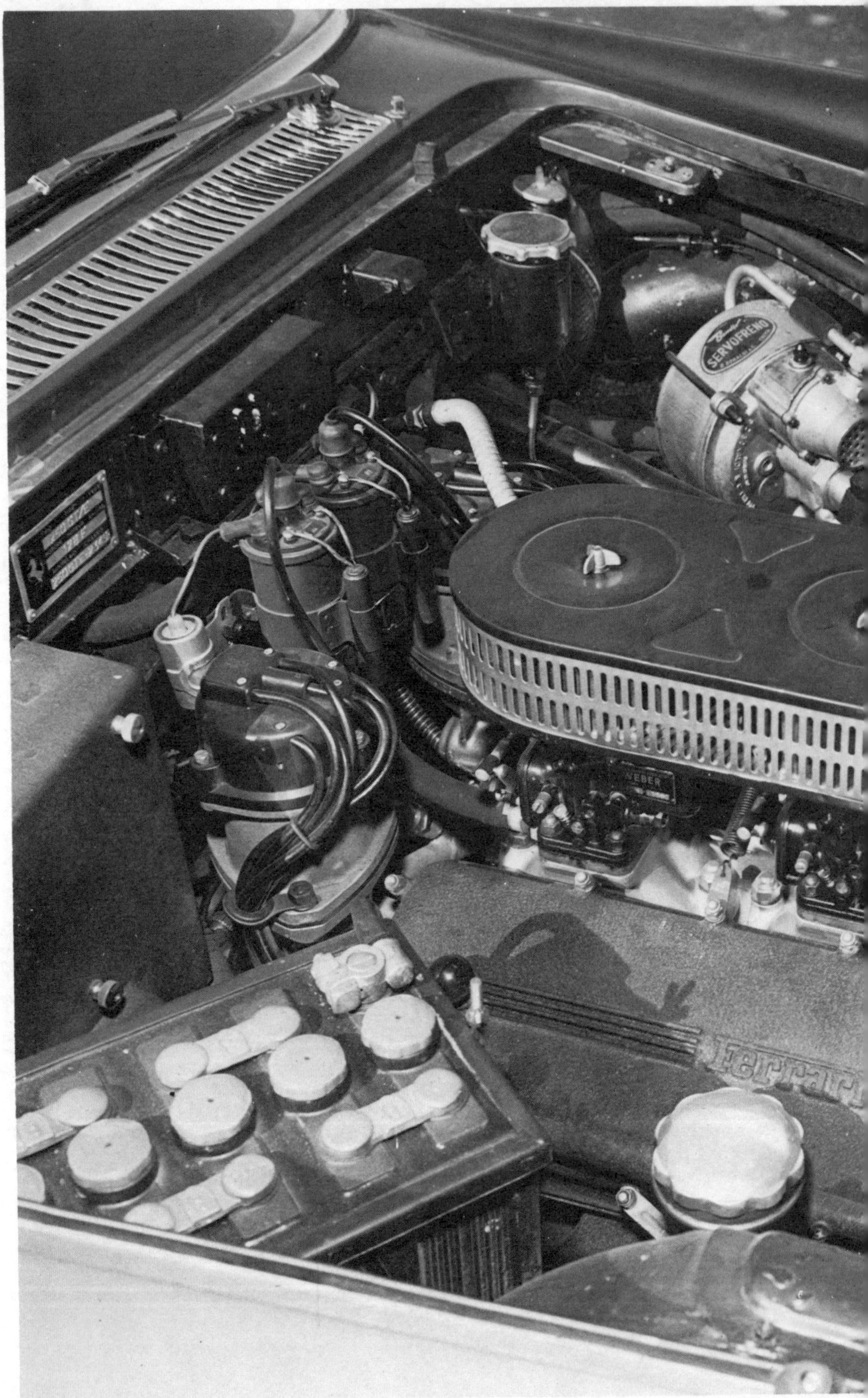
SERVOFRENO
WEBER

In the engine compartment of the 250GT there is plenty of beautiful detailing, as for instance the water plumbing at the right of the picture

reheated and tweaked to give the appropriate angular interval. This is done by BSA and Triumph for their three-cylinder motor cycles, for example, and is also done to the crankshafts of certain high-performance automotive diesels. The trouble in Ferrari's case is that the tradition of the polished shaft carved from solid steel is now firmly established as an inalienable feature of the Ferrari engine, and any departure from this tradition might be interpreted as a cheapening of the car and a lowering of the standards to which it is manufactured.

Ferrari are not averse to using machinery where it can do a particular job well. Such a machine is that which grinds all twelve lobes of a camshaft at once, a vast improvement in timing accuracy and manufacturing economy over the old system whereby the cams were ground one at a time. But this machine cannot be kept working to capacity in the Ferrari factory: generally it works only one day in four. However if Ferrari think they can do better by going to an outside supplier for a component than by making it themselves, they will do so.

Their steering mechanisms provide an interesting example, because production Ferraris have kept the old worm-and-peg steering box despite a general increase in the popularity of the rack-and-pinion. This is a Continental fashion, the Italians in particular having succeeded in producing good steering with the worm-and-peg and related mechanisms when nobody else seems able to do so. It does prompt lurking suspicions that the steering geometry contains imperfections which could produce uncomfortable wheelfight if a rack-and-pinion system were used. But since many Ferraris, including some of the latest, steer with such commendable smoothness and precision through their worm-and-peg arrangements, such suspicions are uncharitable. If something can be as good as that, why alter it – especially when cheapness is not a prime requisite?

If cheapness was an object, Ferrari would presumably buy everything from outside suppliers anyway – the engine first of all; but what problems they would have to face instead! They could not possibly be as flexible as they are. Suppose they went to an outside supplier for a component: the contractor would probably want six months for design work, and another six for tooling. In that same year Ferrari with their own resources and facilities could have their own component in production.

The gearbox is a good example. If instead of making their own, which incorporates Porsche synchromesh, Ferrari were to buy the gearbox from ZF, the only manufacturers providing a range containing anything really suitable, they would have to take the production ZF five-speeder. Ferrari would have to take the gate layout as it was, whether they liked it or not. Then, if they wanted to alter a gear ratio because it did not suit their requirements they might have to wait six months because ZF would have to design the other gears, start making them, feed them into the Ferrari consignment of boxes, and then transport them to Italy and clear Customs. Parkes said on this very point: 'It all adds up to problems, not that we are not prepared to face them if the rewards are there. I have been rather disappointed, frankly, because obviously I have been keen to see English products on the Ferrari car from specialist suppliers who can make the things, probably better than we can make them ourselves. But in spite of the talk about export drives and so on, I was let down so often with promises and deliveries for things we had asked for that I just had to give up completely. Anyway, if there is a locally-made product available, you take it because you can go and fetch it if there is any trouble and you get the thing thrashed out much more quickly and effectively.'

This do-it-yourself approach can introduce other problems of a critical nature, problems which are not always appreciated by the small but expanding specialist manufacturer. Many would-be rivals of Ferrari have fallen by the wayside due to inadequate spares and service facilities, which might supposedly be made easier if (to take an hypothetical case) the Ferrari had the same gearbox as a Jaguar. But would the Ferrari customer know? If he had gearbox trouble he would be more likely to go to the Ferrari agent, who in turn would buy from the factory a spare Ferrari gearbox. Rationally and economically, the sense in utilising other people's products is incontestable; but when you look at the philosophy and psychology of the motor car and especially at the psychology of cus-

Top: Few but fine were the bodies built by Bertone on the 250GT. This is the inside of one of the last. Above: For a different type of driver, this 1961 interior sports two chronographs but no speedometer

tomers who spend vast amounts of money on a car, the realisation comes that the obvious way is not always the best way of doing things. It all comes back to the point that if everything possible is made under one roof, control over it all is complete. This is the essence of Ferrari manufacturing philosophy.

33

THE FRONT ENGINED SINGLE SEATERS

A Ferrari is nothing without its engine and the engine would be nothing without its racing background. The layman may see the ordinary road-going production Ferrari as a racing machine in disguise, but the enthusiast sees it as a means of subsidising the factory's racing team. Despite the expensive processes by which road-going Ferrari cars are produced, it has been estimated that their elevated price gives Ferrari a profit margin of about one hundred per cent, and indeed there have been embittered rivals who have estimated the margin as considerably higher. But this profit is necessary because motor racing is an inordinately expensive business, and Ferrari has engaged in it, despite all his threats of withdrawal, continuously since 1949. His devotion to the sport has led him to maintain a team in the highest class of racing, namely, Grand Prix events for single-seater cars.

This is not to dismiss his efforts in sports car racing, which from time to time have sustained his reputation during periods of dismal failure in Grands Prix. Such periods have been frequent and sometimes lengthy; but even when Ferrari's single-seater fortunes have been at their nadir, his entries have always been welcomed in Formula 1 and Formula 2 racing.

Ever since 1949 the commercialism of motor racing has grown apace so that the Formula 1 Ferrari team, still having about it the air that was once common to all the great factory teams, appears progressively more distinguished by its curiously aloof and aristocratic tone. Behind the scenes Ferrari has shown himself on many occasions to be as shrewd and avaricious as any of his rivals; but overtly the Ferrari team is less commercial than the others and therefore to be respected even when its performance is not to be feared.

In twenty-four years of Grand Prix racing by Ferrari cars, fortune has

The blown 1½-litre V12 at the 1950 Swiss GP

shown them distinct favour only in 1949, 1951, 1952, 1953, 1956, 1961, 1964 and in the latter part of 1970. On the other hand we may remember such catastrophic years as 1955, 1960, 1962, 1967, 1968, and 1969, when nothing that they did seemed to be right and every imaginable accusation of obstinacy, incompetence, senescence and spitefulness was flung against the old man whose name has been associated with and represented in racing for far more years than that of anybody else in the whole world.

When the time comes, as some day it must, for Ferrari's contribution to motor racing to be summarised, it will not be the cars, the arguments, the triumphs, the games of bluff, nor the parade of associated famous names that will be seen to have most distinguished his career. Pride of place will be given to the courageous and enduring spirit by which he has been moved. Nevertheless it is worth looking at the cars with which he has gone campaigning in single-seater racing, for they constitute an astonishingly large family. It is all very well for Bugatti type numbers to run into the sixties and Lotus into the seventies, but both these lists are characterised by the sort of finickiness that would consider allocating a new type number in the event of some bit of a car falling off. By contrast, Ferrari single-seater racing cars number over fifty distinct types, after discounting all the myriad minor alterations to which almost every one of them was subjected in the course of its racing career.

This is a remarkable number, representing as it does more than two distinct new designs for every year in which the Ferrari company has been engaged in racing. A few of these cars have been Formula 2 models, and there have been one or two isolated instances of specials being built for Indianapolis, for the Tasman series of races held in Australia and New Zealand, and for one or two private owners who, though they were not fully aware of it, were acting as guinea

Above: Luigi Villoresi in one of the early Lampredi cars, the big unblown V12 of 1950.
Right: The air collector box for the carburettors of Lampredi's first big unblown engine were typical of early Ferrari practice.

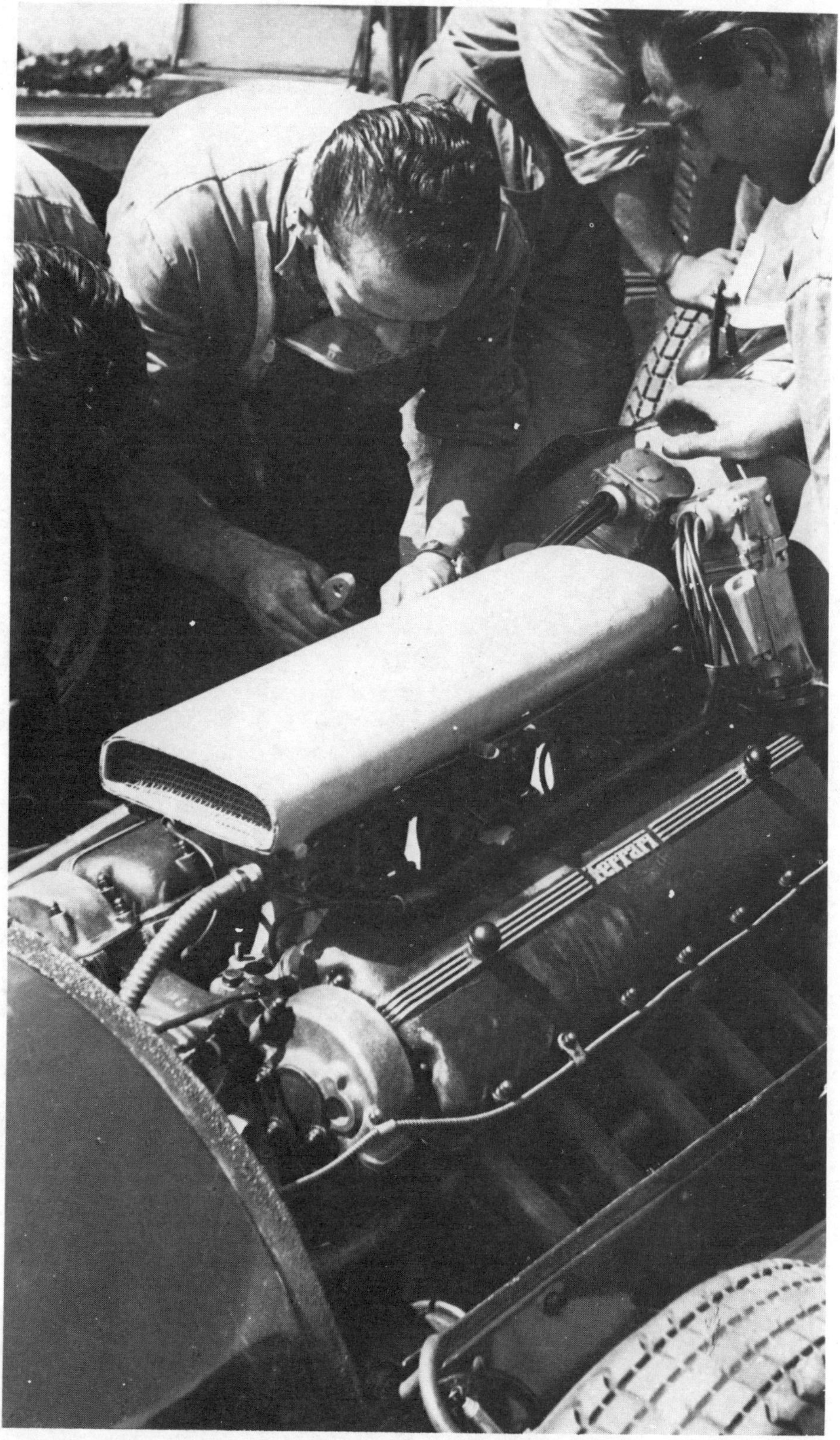
Ferrari

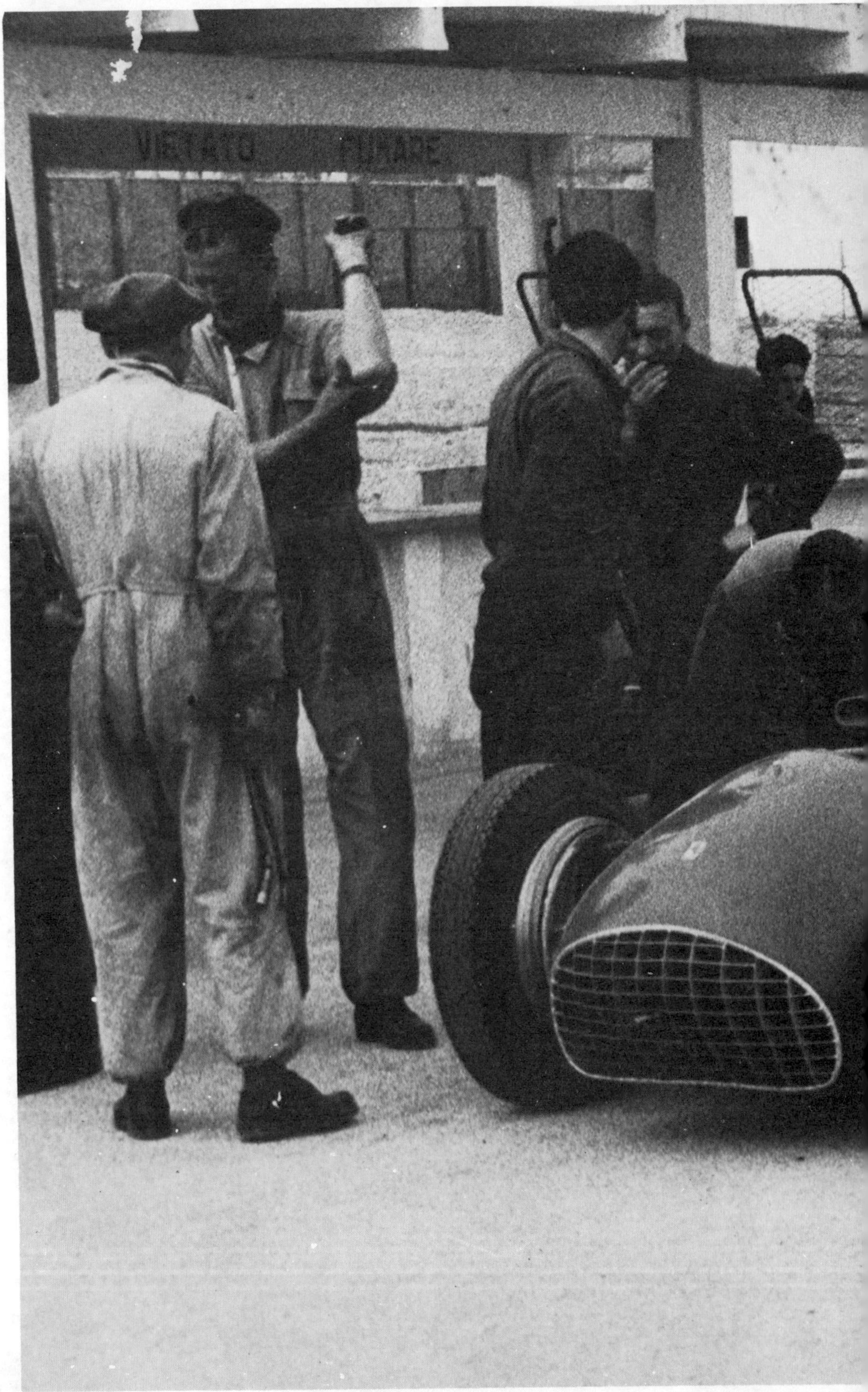
VIETATO FUMARE

When the unblown V12 grew to its full 4½-litres, it was at last competitive. Here it is in the pits before the 1951 German GP . . .

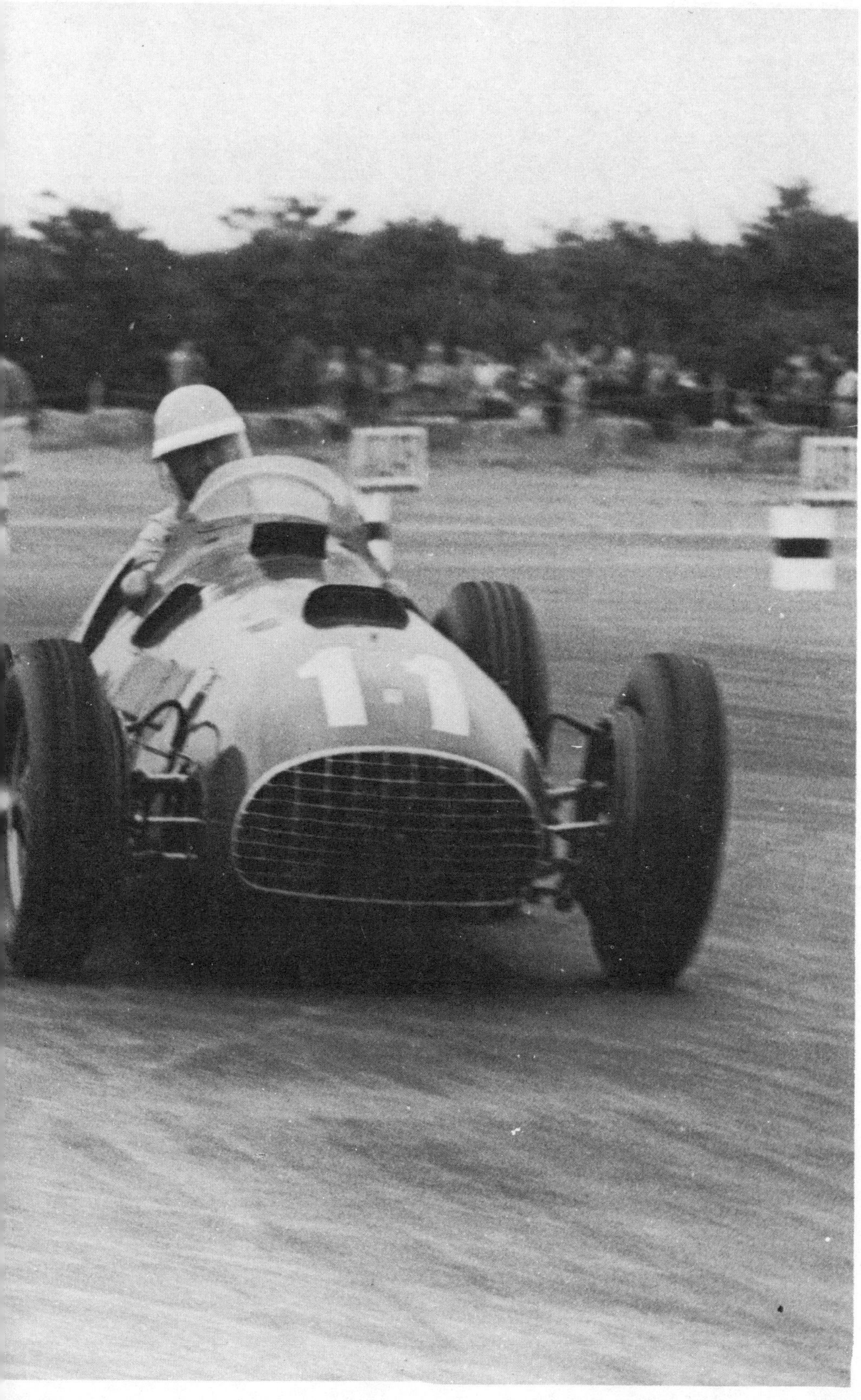

The 4½ litre V12 cars in echelon at the Silverstone pits in 1951

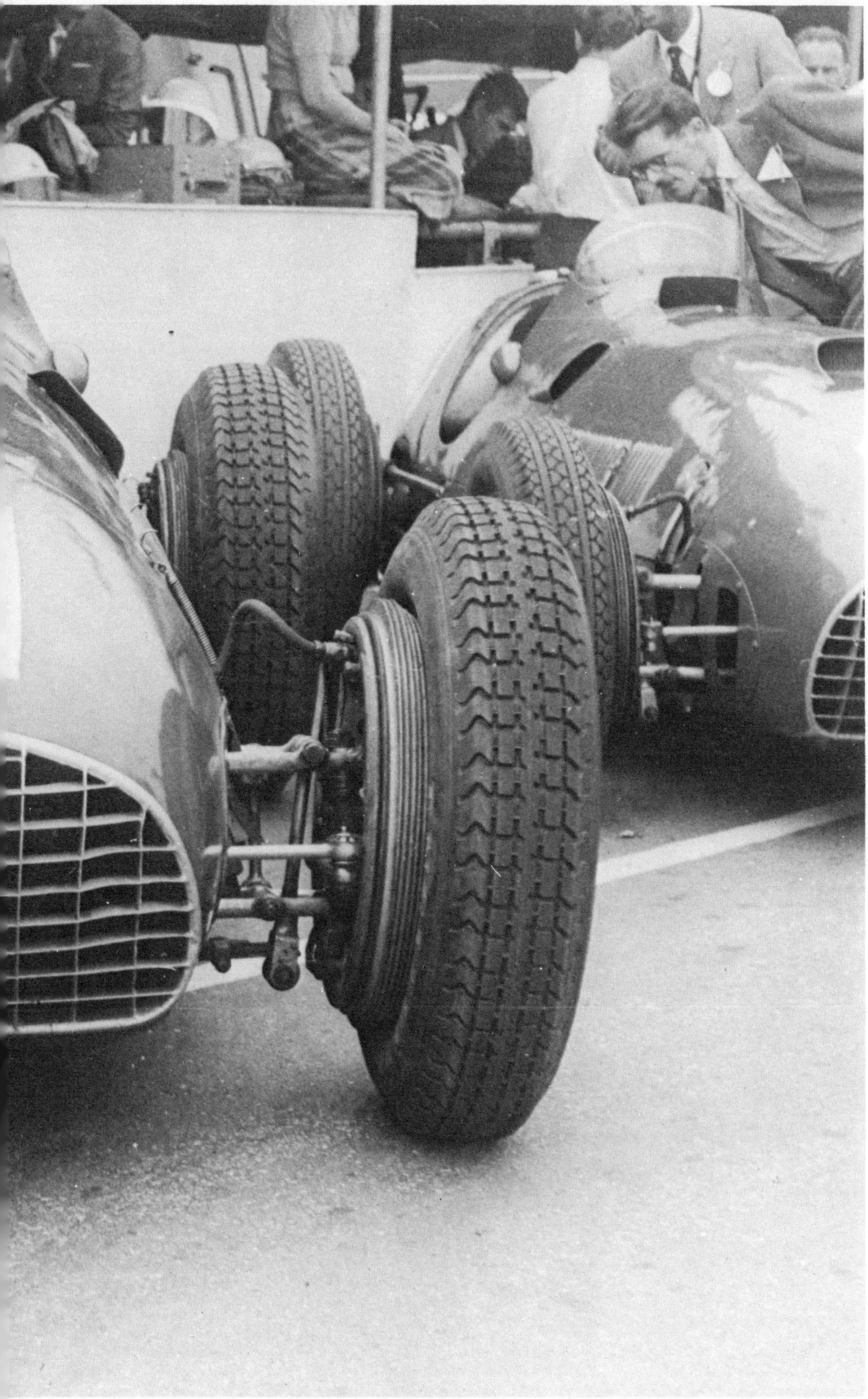

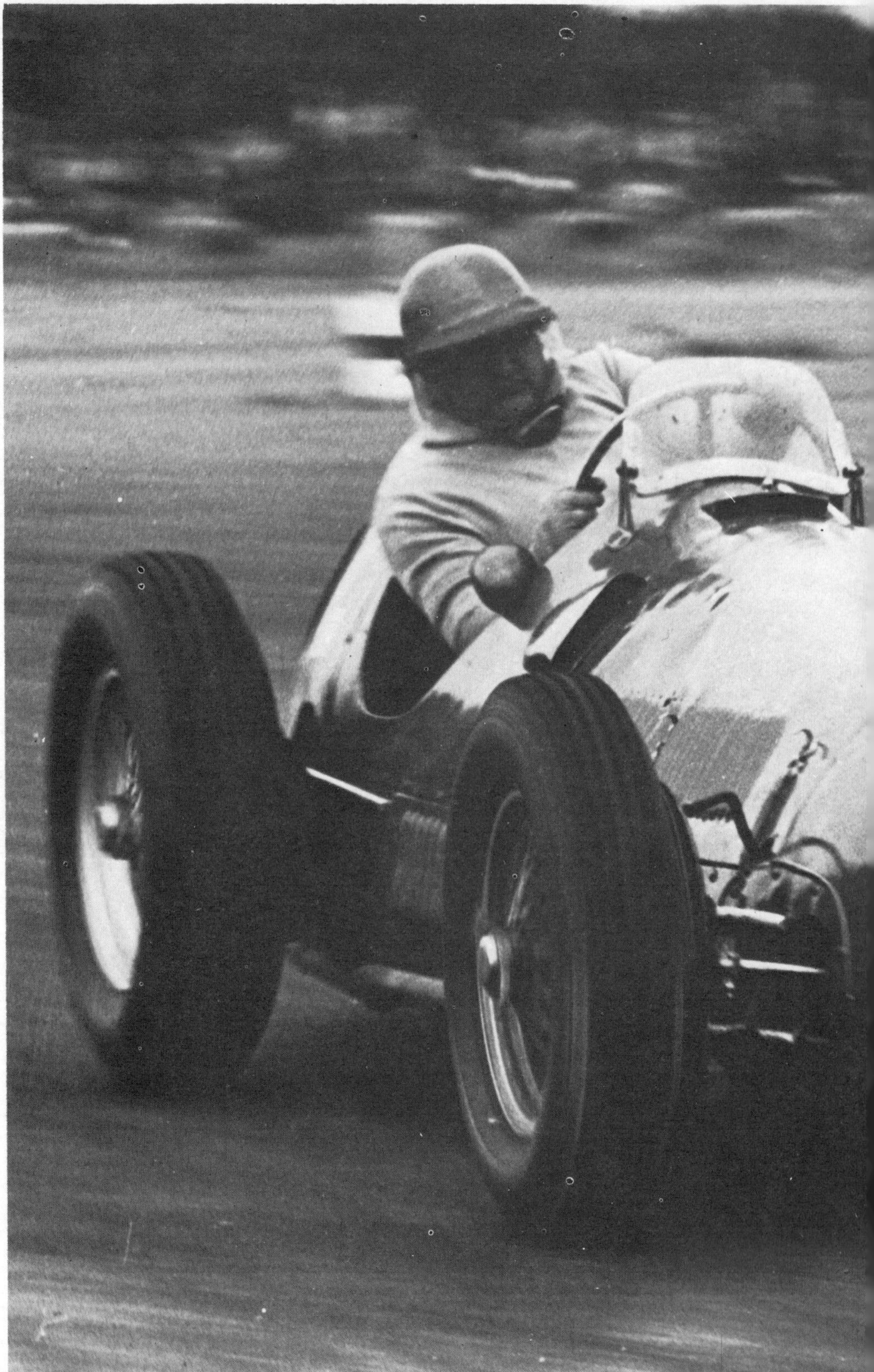

... and during the race, driven by Villoresi

pigs in the Ferrari development programme. Discounting such specials (for example the unsupercharged 2½ litre swing-axle car built for the Swiss driver Fischer as a prelude to the introduction of the big unblown Lampredi V12 of 1950) there have been eighteen basic types of Ferrari single-seaters in Grand Prix racing since 1947. They range in engine capacity from 1½ to 4½ litres, in power output from under 140bhp to over 460, and in track from less than four feet to more than five feet. Nearly every one of them won something, and some of them won nearly everything.

The first was hardly conceived as a Grand Prix car at all. It was the type 159, virtually a bored-out version of the original post-war type 125, whose V12 engine was designed by Colombo to have a capacity of 1½-litres, increased to 1.9-litres in the case of the type 159. The chassis was a simple tubular structure adapted to a live rear axle and independent front suspension by wishbones and transverse spring, and the late Raymond Sommer drove one of these cars to victory in the Turin GP of 1947, establishing in the course of the race a new record lap.

It was splendid, but it was not a real racing car. The first of these followed in 1948. It followed Alfa Romeos, it followed Maseratis; and when it was not chasing these it was chasing its own tail, for it had been given all-independent suspension by the simple and altogether too popular expedient of mounting the final drive casing at the rear of the chassis and pivoting from it two swinging half-axles. In a distressingly large number of examples before the war but most vividly in the Auto Unions and certain Alfa Romeos, such a layout had shown itself to produce a violent and scarcely controllable oversteering characteristic, due to the high roll centre and extreme camber variations implicit in its geometry. Yet here was a Ferrari with a wheelbase only 85 inches long, looking rather high and stubby and with its rear wheels point-

Above: The most famous and important of all Ferrari's GP victories was in 1951 when Froilan Gonzales, in this 1950 4½-litre car at the British GP, gave Alfa Romeo their first post-war defeat. Below: In 1952, GP racing was in the doldrums. Britain put on a F1 race at Boreham, and Villoresi won it in this 4½-litre V12 with enlarged carburettor air intake

Luigi Villoresi, in the spring of 1951

Lorenzo Bandini

Fangio

ing in every conceivable direction on their swing axles while trying to transmit the 225bhp which single-stage supercharging was reputed to have produced from the original 1½-litre engine.

This car, the type 125 Gran Premio, was announced in the winter of 1946-47, at the same time as the sporting and competition versions of the type 125; and as well as presaging a glorious succession of Ferraris with which the roads and race tracks of Europe and the world might be graced, it also made some interesting moves towards future practice at a time when most other racing cars – and certainly the successful ones – adhered firmly to principles established before the war. For example it ran on 15-inch wheels instead of the customary 17-inch size. and its engine relied almost entirely on steel-backed thin-wall plain bearings rather than the ball or roller bearings which had been considered desirable or even essential in classical racing

Before the 1951 German GP, Villoresi (right) and Alberto Ascari (centre) confer with designer Aurelio Lampredi

engines. This was the car which had been designed by Colombo with a view to making Ferrari competitive in a class of racing in which the type 158 Alfa Romeo, designed before the war by the same man, was still pre-eminent. Colombo knew that he had to beat the Alfa, and so did Ferrari: and since they had both worked on the design and development of the Alfa when they had been in the service of the Milanese firm in 1938, they ought to have known what they were up against.

Yet they failed to do so, and it is interesting to consider the reasons for their failure which persisted until 1951. The car's first outing in the 1948 Italian Grand Prix, run in pouring rain, was perhaps its best, for Sommer drove closely in the wake of the leading Alfa Romeo for much of the race and succeeded in finishing third. It won races later, but never ones in which the redoubtable Alfa Romeos were running; and at the end of 1948 Alfa Romeo decided that there was no point in racing all the time against unworthy opposition and withdrew from the lists for the following season. In their absence this little Ferrari was the most successful Grand Prix car of 1949, judged on the basis of the results in the Grandes Epreuves; but the performances it achieved were always of a lower standard than had been set by the Alfas in the past. The most that could be said about the car was that it was very promising. When it followed the example set by its unsupercharged Formula 2 version and its wheelbase was lengthened by six inches to improve the handling, it began to look as though some of this promise might actually be realised.

To the student of engine design, however, the great disappointment remained the rather poor performance of the engine when related to the potential that seemed to be there. It was by the standards of its time a remarkable engine, having an exceptionally large piston area resulting

Paul Frere, on his home ground for the 1955 Belgian GP at Spa, drove one of the Ferrari team Supersquali

from the large number of cylinders, each with bore appreciably larger than stroke. Indeed, this Colombo design was the first Grand Prix engine since 1907 with a bore larger than its stroke. When considered according to any of the generally accepted mechanical limits, such as those imposed by mean piston velocity or maximum piston acceleration, this engine should have been capable of running at 10,000 rpm and exploiting its potentially good breathing to develop close to 300 bhp with single-stage boost. But this never happened. The maximum engine speed was no more than 7,500 rpm and the bmep was disappointingly low; both failings presumably attributable to the porting or to some mechanical limitations imposed by the valve operating gear, which consisted basically of a single overhead camshaft to each bank of cylinders, operating the inclined valves through rockers. However, this limited performance was sufficient to win the day when the Alfas were not there, despite the fact that the Ferrari engine rating did not bear comparison with what had been achieved before the war.

During the 1949 season Ascari and Villoresi drove it to victory on a number of occasions, although losing to an unsupercharged Talbot in the Belgian Grand Prix due to having to refuel while the relatively abstemious French car was able to continue non-stop – a lesson which Ferrari took to heart and was never to forget.

The successor to this car made its first appearance for the Italian Grand Prix at Monza towards the end of the 1949 season. The engine was basically still the Colombo V12; but it now had two gear-driven camshafts to each cylinder head, and its power output was increased to 305bhp with the assistance of two-stage supercharging

Its track was widened from 47 to 50 inches and the whole car was lower and leaner than its predecessor. Driven by Ascari, it led the race from start to finish.

In 1950 it had the Alfa Romeo team to contend with, which put a rather different complexion on things. Even when Ferrari fielded the strongest possible team, comprising Ascari and Villoresi with the two-stage cars and Sommer and others with the earlier models, as at San Remo, the Alfa Romeos simply romped away. There seemed little more that Ferrari could do with these cars. They could not hold the Alfas along the straight and were still rather difficult around corners. An attempt to improve the handling was made in time for the Swiss GP at Berne when the new car appeared in a modified form, the swing axle rear suspension being replaced by a De Dion system, accompanied by a reduction in wheelbase of two inches. It was hardly an auspicious introduction, for the axle of one car broke and the other car went out with engine trouble.

Colombo went out too. He insisted that the way to success was in further development of the highly supercharged engine, a theory to which the majority of contemporary designers would have subscribed. Assisting Colombo on the Ferrari staff however was Lampredi, who maintained with equal vigour the argument that an unsupercharged engine of $4\frac{1}{2}$-litres capacity, as permitted by the regulations, could give as much power as was necessary to equal the performance of the smaller supercharged machine while using less fuel. This would mean freedom from refuelling stops and from the prejudicial effect on handling of a substantial fuel load which diminished during the course of a race making it impossible to achieve

Farina's Supersqualo shows its chrome 'sighting line' along the bonnet

Above: In 1953 the classic races were again run by F2 cars, and the Ferrari with its four-cylinder Lampredi engine was almost invincible. The loss of a wheel can, however, be a serious handicap. Below: Showing more typical form, Ascari in the 2-litre F2 Ferrari wins the 1953 British GP. Here he is lapping the Maserati of Felice Bonnetto

Above: Ascari again, in the Type 500 with which he had such a brilliant season in 1953 Below: Jano's V8 Lancia, as extensively amended by Ferrari for 1956, negotiating the paddock for the British GP of that year

a satisfactory compromise in such matters as tyre pressures, spring rates, damper settings and the like. Ferrari himself, remembering the success of the Talbot at Spa, sided with Lampredi. Considering what Colombo's design had achieved for him in the past couple of years, it was ungrateful of him not to retain Colombo's services – though as we shall see, it was Colombo's engine design that was to bring Ferrari more consistent glory than any other. Lampredi was given his opportunity, and he seized it avidly.

Although he knew from the outset that he was allowed 4½ litres, Lampredi made his initial unblown 'big banger' a V12 of only 3.3 litres. This engine was inserted in the chassis of the two-stage de Dion car and was run experimentally in the Belgian GP on 18th June 1950. It was not very fast, despite the efforts of Ascari who was twelve seconds slower in his best practice lap than the fastest Alfa Romeo, and two seconds slower than the fastest six-cylinder Talbot. Late the following month, however, when the car reappeared for the GP des Nations at Geneva, Lampredi had exploited his best design feature – cylinder liners screwed into the head – to enlarge the bore to give a capacity of 4.1 litres. In practice the car was now two seconds a lap slower than the best of the Alfas and four seconds faster than the Talbot.

For the Italian GP in September Lampredi, having already increased the 72 millimetres bore to 80 millimetres, now extended the 68 millimetre stroke to 74.5, achieving a final 4.5 litres. From this came 330bhp, soon to be increased to 380 when the ignition was duplicated, and this power was realised at 7500 rpm – a rate as high, be it noted, as could be sustained by the Colombo 1½-litre engine in its original form.

Ferrari relied upon this car for the Monza race which brought the 1950 season towards its close. When the car led briefly from Farina's Alfa Romeo during the race, Ferrari's faith in an unsupercharged future must have seemed sufficiently vindicated. If, having got the measure of the Alfa Romeo, he entertained any doubts about Britain's fantastic BRM, whose very highly supercharged 16-cylinder 1½-litre engine was the object of so much comment and curiosity, such doubts must have been resolved when the big new Ferrari came home the winner of the Spanish GP at Barcelona, from which Alfa Romeo abstained and in which BRM abjectly failed.

But there were still the Alfa Romeos to be beaten. Throughout the first half of the 1951 season the Ferrari team continued, now with twin ignition, improved brakes, and steadily improving morale. Then at Silverstone in midsummer came that epoch making British Grand Prix when Gonzales started the big Ferrari on pole position on the grid and the cat was well and truly among the pigeons. He had earned his place with a lap at over 100mph, the first ever achieved on the Silverstone circuit and done in a time that was a clear second better than Fangio could achieve as leader of the Alfa Romeo team.

What a race that was! There have been many others since as exciting, and as important in human terms: Fangio in the German GP at the Nurburgring in 1957, Moss winning there and at Monaco in 1961, or Clark excelling himself at Monza in 1968. But there has not been another race to compare with this one for historical importance. A kindly oblivion has removed the recollection of many a subsequent race of equal status, but twenty years have not dimmed my memory of that Homeric struggle between two Argentinian drivers in two Italian cars fighting tooth and nail for mastery and leaving Ascari, Villoresi, Farina, the BRMs and history behind. There were times when Gonzales, who was driving a 1950 Ferrari while his team mates had 1951 models, seemed just a little too wild to be good. But when Fangio had to stop for fuel Gonzales knew that his race was as good as won. Thereafter it was Fangio whose driving assumed an air of desperation, and he finished a minute behind the Ferrari. Ascari's gearbox went, but Villoresi brought the other Ferrari into third place in front of the remaining Alfas. Since 1923, when Fiat introduced it, the supercharger had been the god of Grand Prix motor racing. Now after twenty-eight years here was another Italian to preach a new faith.

It could have been just a flash in the pan, but it was not. In the German GP, only Fangio's Alfa Romeo was able to punctuate a finishing order in which the 4½-litre Ferraris occupied 1st, 3rd, 4th and 5th places. At Bari where they next met, Fangio beat the Ferraris. At Monza it looked as though the Ferrari trio would thrash the Alfas again. Then suddenly Farina turned on a tremendous 'tigering' display which might have altered things if he had not had to stop for fuel, finishing third. Lastly came the Barcelona race. Ascari's Ferrari was 1½ seconds faster than Fangio's Alfa in practice. In the race the boot was on the other foot and the Ferrari team, plagued by unsatisfactory tyres, was a complete shambles and was lucky to net a second place. The world championship went to Fangio, and Alfa Romeo were cock-a-hoop. Or so it seemed; maybe they were just delighted at the opportunity to get out while the going was good and while they still had some face, for they took the opportunity to announce their withdrawal from racing.

Alfa Romeo could afford to be content with what they had achieved, which was nothing less than the complete domination of Grand Prix racing for more than five years and in twenty-five successive races, a period of ascendancy such as has been achieved by no other single model. However, most people at the end of 1951 accepted that Alfa Romeo had been beaten in fair fight by Ferrari, and the Barcelona event was dismissed as an exception to the rule that it is the last battle which wins the war. Alfa Romeo domination had been broken, of that there was no doubt. Similarly there was no doubt that his success in breaking it gave Ferrari more personal satisfaction than anything he had done before, and possibly more than anything he has achieved since. Ferrari is a proud man.

Yet he would not have much to be proud of in the future if there was to be no worthy opposition to his big battle wagons. Talbots and Maseratis were mere chaff, and no race promoter was going to risk relying on the intransigent BRM to provide the Ferraris with regular worthwhile opposition throughout the following season. So it was decided that in 1952 and 1953 the drivers' world championship would be decided on the basis of performances in Formula 2 racing. Technically the Formula 1 for Grands Prix must endure, but in practice nobody was going to bother. Certainly, nobody was going to devise an expensive new car just for the sake of seeing the old formula out. There would be a few formule libre short distance affairs for occasions of minor importance, but the classics would all be Formula 2 affairs.

It was blue-eyed Lampredi's job to provide Ferrari with a suitable car. He did it in the traditional Italian way, by copying an existing chassis and putting a beautiful new engine in it.

Lampredi's choice of a simple four-cylinder engine for this new car, which became known as type 500, seemed a terrible regression to many people at the time, but we must consider what requirements he had to satisfy. Formula 2, as then constituted, required a single-seater racing car with an unsupercharged engine of not more than 2-litres swept volume, and in the past few years Ferrari had campaigned with a fair degree of success with the 2-litre version of the original Colombo V12. By 1950 this was giving about 170bhp and in that year the chassis was revised, with de Dion suspension at the rear and a longer wheelbase. Only once in that year did it fail to make the fastest lap (at Rome) and only once in that year did it fail to win (at Geneva).

But in 1951 the opposition presented by the Simca Gordini and to a lesser extent by the HWM made it clear that

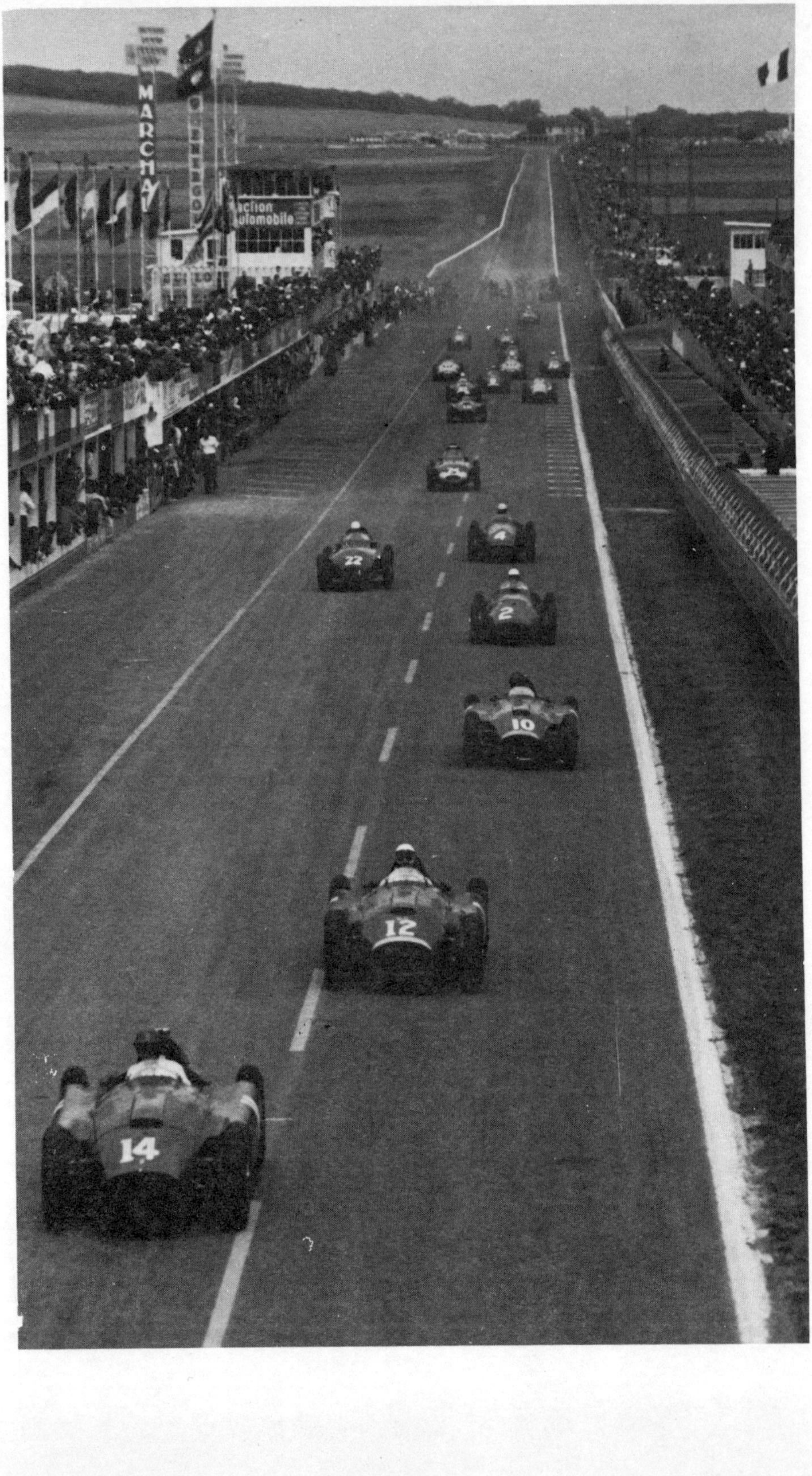
Automobile
22
4
2
10
12
14

Ferrari could not safely rely on this design for the following years when so much more would be at stake. Other rivals were known to be in the offing, most notably the fast and powerful six-cylinder Maserati to which Columbo and Massimino were devoting their attentions. From Britain the HWM was being followed by the Connaught, the Cooper and the G-type ERA, the last two relying for motive power on the rather old-fashioned but often surprising Bristol engine, whose outstanding volumetric efficiency was often lost beneath a forest of pushrods. Yet volumetric efficiency promised to be the key note of all new unsupercharged designs. The realisation was spreading among car designers, from the motorcyling fraternity whose racing engines had exploited the principle for many years, that much was to be gained by the provision of a separate carburettor choke and inlet tract for each cylinder. If this sort of induction system were combined with an exhaust system that was similarly contrived to exploit resonances and ram effects through the engine's alimentary canal, then cylinder filling could be improved enormously. To achieve this in an engine of many cylinders would be difficult. To develop such an inlet and exhaust system for a four-cylinder, or at most a six-cylinder, engine would obviously be easier than to do so for an eight or twelve. Besides, the bulk and weight penalty of a dozen carburettors and associate plumbing had to be taken into account together with the inevitably greater weight of a multi-cylindered engine anyway. Furthermore the comparatively small companies now engaged in motor racing, such as Ferrari, could ill afford to maintain a full team of cars with very complex engines in face

Left: At the start of the 1956 French GP at Heims, the Ferrari trio leads away. The Vanwalls lying fifth and seventh are just straws in the wind. Below: The Ferrari V8 in its champ -ionship-winning year, here appear -ing to understeer strongly at Spa

of the increasing congestion in the international racing calendar. So simplicity of design had further advantages in practice that might not be apparent in theory.

To Lampredi's credit, he recognised all these influences, and despite the success with which he had established himself as a designer through the medium of the unsupercharged V12 engine, he had the courage not to repeat himself but to strike out afresh. What he produced was a four-cylinder engine of supreme beauty, an engine whose major castings had a fluidity of contour which bore witness to the elegant solution of many problems of stress distribution. As in his big V12, Lampredi made use of cylinder liners which were screwed into the cylinder head combustion chamber. This eliminated the conventional combustion restraining gasket, simplified the shaping and scavenging of the cooling water passages (especially those critical ones around the exhaust ports and spark plug bosses) and facilitated the close pitching of the cylinder centres which in turn allowed the construction of a short engine with a torsionally stiff crankshaft.

This beautiful structure was surmounted by a twin-camshaft cylinder head in which the two imposing inclined valves were controlled by hairpin springs. Between valve and cam was a

At Monza for the 1956 Italian GP, the Ferrari team was still committed to Englebert tyres

light-alloy tubular tappet independently controlled by two coil springs so as to keep its surmounted roller follower in contact with the cam. Two twin choke Weber carburettors and two pairs of tuned exhaust pipes provided the necessary deep breathing, and in one hundred days from the time that Lampredi started work on the design, the engine was finished and capable of producing 160bhp. This was soon increased to 180 at 7,000 rpm equivalent to a bmep of 11.8 atmospheres (165 lb/in^2). Thus were his theories confirmed, for this mean effective pressure was fourteen per cent higher than in the 2-litre V12, and the power output was at least comparable despite a more modest piston area. The new engine was lighter and had a broader spread of useful power, making it feasible to rely on a four-speed gearbox instead of the five-speeder that had been invariably associated with the unblown 2-litre V12.

Of course the expected opposition materialised. The Maserati was undoubtedly very fast and its leading exponent was no less than Fangio, who alone at the time could be considered the equal in driving ability and track craft of Ferrari's leading driver Ascari. Then there was the sensational appearance of the Bristol-engined Cooper in the hands of the hitherto unknown Hawthorn, who was destined to become world famous within a year and to lead the Ferrari team. The new six-cylinder Gordini had also to be reckoned with and indeed one of these beat Ferrari on the very fast Reims circuit in 1952. But this was the only defeat suffered by the Ferrari team during the year, the results otherwise proving the combination of Ascari and Ferrari to be invincible.

In 1953 the results were almost as monotonous, although the actual racing was frequently exciting due to the doughty opposition presented by Maserati. There were times when they were significantly faster, but proved less reliable, as in the Belgian and French Grand Prix. It was in the French race that Hawthorn, in a works Ferrari, challenged and beat Fangio. He fought him all the way and eventually led him over the finishing line by a mere second after two-and-three-quarter hours racing at an average speed of over 113mph. The Ferrari had handled better and the Maserati suffered a severe caning of the brakes in Fangio's effort to compensate for this shortcoming; and towards the end Fangio lost second gear. Nevertheless Hawthorn's was a masterly drive and it postponed until the Italian GP at Monza the day when Ferrari would finally be beaten, this time by Fangio with the scarcely more comfortable lead of 1.4 seconds at the finish. The dominant Ferrari failed to win its last race.

In 1954 the new Formula 1 came into

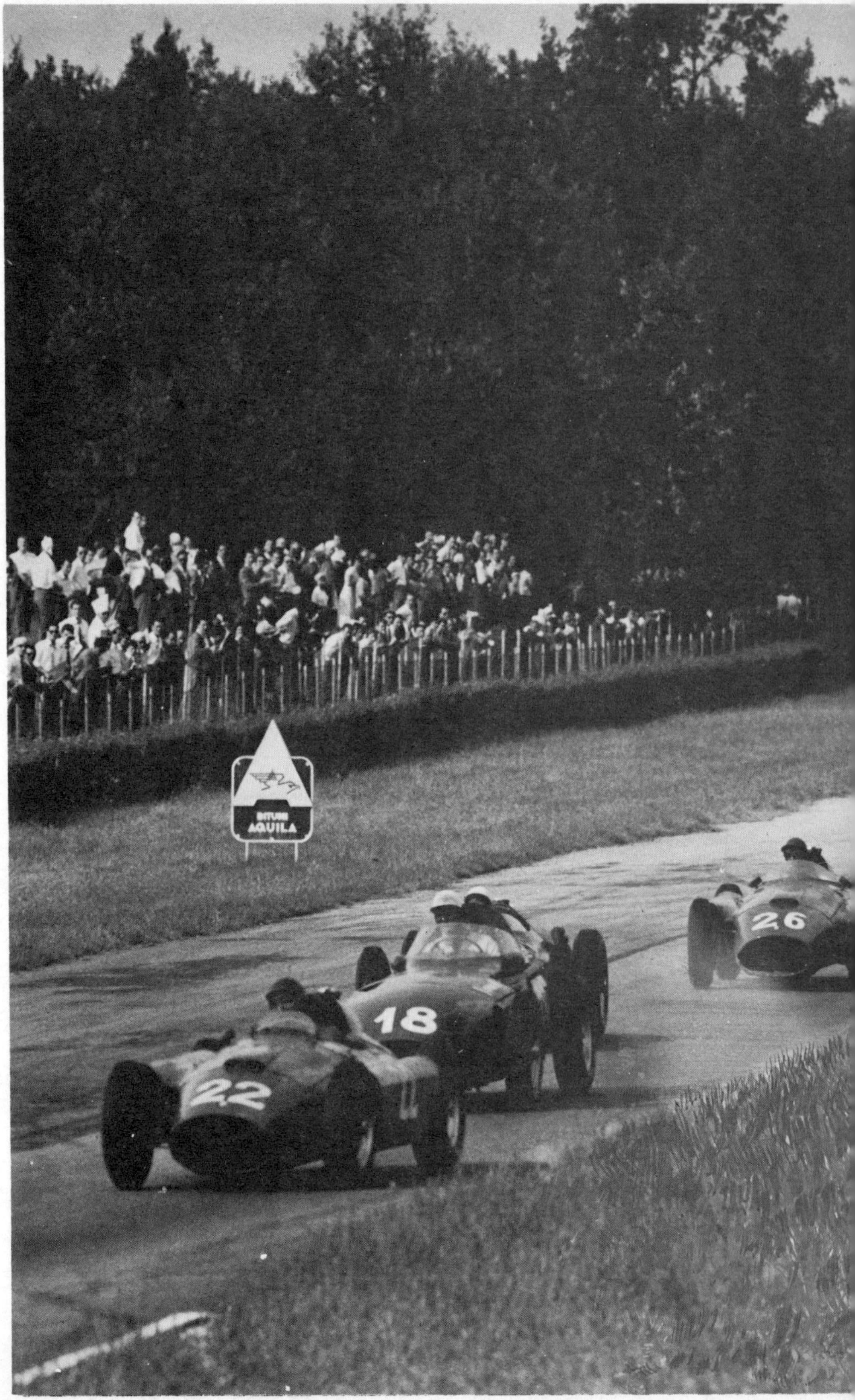
AQUILA
18
22
26

effect, permitting unsupercharged cars of 2½-litres or supercharged ones of a mere ¾-litre. It introduced a period of six years in which the racing public saw a succession of technically novel and morphologically varied cars. These cars succeeded each other in a way which allowed none to retain supremacy for long. This period, from 1954 to 1960, can fairly be judged one of the golden ages of motor racing; but there was only one manufacturer whose cars were active throughout the period, and that was Ferrari.

When the time came to determine the design of the 1954 Formula 1 car, Lampredi must have felt justified in developing his existing type 500 Formula 2 car. Indeed it would have been difficult for him to argue any other case: for as Aristotle observed, the test of truth in matters of practice is to be found in the results obtained, for it is only in them that supreme authority resides. The results obtained by the type 500 Ferrari in the series of races for the world championship in 1952 and 1953 were paralysingly authoritarian. So it was only to be expected that the 1954 GP Ferrari should bear a strong resemblance to its predecessor, for 2-litres is not so much less than 2½-litres as to justify a revolution in the drawing office.

Daimler-Benz and Lancia might well come up with something different in time, but when the season opened Ferrari were there with the new type 625 car, strongly resembling the type 500. Its engine was of course of a full 2½-litres capacity, and the more recent chassis was based on a multiplicity of tubes rather than on the simple almost ladder-like pattern of the earlier car. The four cylinders each had a gargan-

As always at Monza, the pace in 1956 was killing. Here are Fangio, 1956 World Champion driver (number 22), leading Schell (Vanwall, 18), Moss (Maserati, beyond Schell). Collins (Ferrari, 25) and Baron de Graffenreid (Maserati 14, a lap behind) past the abandoned Gordini of Manzon. Moss was the winner...

... and here is one reason why Castelotti was not: one of those troublesome Engleberts fails at 170 mph on the Monza banking. This car was built specially for the 1957 Tasman Series, and shows how Ferrari thought a racing car should look when not inherited from Lancia

tuan bore of 100 millimetres. Huge pistons with a 79½ millimetre stroke limited the engine to 7,200 rev/min, a thousand less than the rival six-cylinder Colombo–designed Maserati could safely reach. When the two cars first met at Buenos Aires for the Argentine GP in January 1954 they tied for fastest practice lap, but it was the Maserati which won the race. Ferraris finished 2nd, 3rd, 4th and 9th. In a minor event at the same venue later in the month it was Trintignant's privately entered Ferrari which won. These two makes fought out all the important races during the first half of that 1954 season, until at the French GP conventions were defied and illusions shattered by the new streamlined W196 Mercedes-Benz with which neither of the Italian cars could seriously contend.

The resounding success of the German cars at Reims made it seem improbable that they would be overcome in the immediate future. But the futility of such forecasts was promptly demonstrated in the next Grande Epreuve at Silverstone when Mercedes-Benz could achieve no better than 4th and 7th places behind two Ferraris and a Maserati. Daimler-Benz did everything possible to ensure that such a disaster should not occur again, least of all in the German GP which figured next on the calendar. They produced apparently new cars with slipper-type bodies replacing the original all-enveloping streamlined shells which had aroused such controversy in the two preceding races. True enough it was a Mercedes-Benz that won – but second and third places were occupied by Ferraris.

These were still the transitional 1953/54 cars, the new short-chassis version being reserved for the future and requiring some further development. Two of the four Ferraris in the German GP had new engines that had been introduced at Rouen a month earlier. These engines had been further modified by relocating the twin magnetos vertically in front of the engine. This was an adaption of the engine of the new Ferrari 750S sports car, another Lampredi design; and indeed the crankcases of the two engines were identical, the GP version even sporting a flange on the timing case for mounting a dynamo. The engine was now remarkably efficient, having been developed in time for this race to give nearly 245bhp and to generate a peak bmep at 5,000 rpm of no less than 207 lb/in^2, a pressure which was considerably higher than that realised in any previous unsupercharged car engine. It was a good example of something simple being made to work well, whereas the Mercedes might have exemplified something complex requiring further development: the difference in power output between the two engines was only 2bhp.

This engine was known as the type 555, and was intended to repose in a different chassis – not entirely new but sufficiently modified to lend the car an air of compactness. It looked lower and was wider amidships where fuel tanks swelled its flanks. The wheelbase was shortened to seven feet, the track was narrower, and the handling was a source of some disappointment, which was why for a long time the 555 engine was raced in the 625 chassis. Even as late as January 1955, this combination was still preferred by most Ferrari drivers, but by then they could seldom entertain any hopes of winning a major race anyway. Hawthorn had won the Spanish GP in the preceding October, driving a 555, with coil springs at the front instead of the usual transverse leaf springs. Mercedes-Benz were forced out by overheating and the new V8 Lancia D50, making its first appearance and proving to be the fastest car there, failed after ten laps.

Hawthorn's Ferrari was the first to be fitted with coil spring suspension, and the modification was accompanied by the fitting of an anti-roll bar at the front. These changes had already given a bonus of three seconds around Monza. Nevertheless 1954 had been a disappointing season for Ferrari.

1955 was even worse. The type 555 had been revised with a new multi-tubular chassis frame, a dilation of the lateral fuel tanks, and a shortening of the tail. So, whereas in 1954, the car had been known as the *Squalo* or Shark, the new version was christened the *Super Squalo*. It proved unpopular, having terribly strong understeer that the drivers found very difficult to overcome on twisty circuits such as Monaco. But it was there that Ferrari scored their only win of the European GP season, Trintignant inheriting first place in his older type 625 model when Mercedes-Benz suffered a rupture of the valve gear and the Lancia of Ascari diverted itself into the harbour.

By the time the Italian GP came round in September, Ascari was dead. Lancia, in severe financial difficulty, had abandoned their racing programme. After a good deal of bickering with Maserati they handed over their cars complete with all spares and designs, not to mention some useful designers and mechanics, to Ferrari. The Maranello concern was happy enough to accept them since it was in the difficult position of having a great reputation to maintain and no car that promised to be capable of doing it. Ferrari presented himself at Monza with three Lancias and three new versions of the Super Squalo which featured five-speed gearboxes among other alterations. In practice everybody had tyre trouble except Mercedes-Benz. The trouble was so severe that the Lancias could not race at all and the Ferraris were not much happier on the dreadful Englebert tyres that had plagued them at various times in previous years. Mercedes finished first and second in their last race. Ferrari and Maserati were all mixed up, with Castelotti taking third place for Ferrari, and everybody else retired.

Probably the most important retirement of all at about this time was that of Lampredi, who left the Ferrari organisation, unhappy at the failure of his more recent cars and doubtless resentful of Ferrari's uncompromising decision to treat him as the scapegoat. The advent of the Lancias and their designer Vittorio Jano left him no room for manoeuvre, and he went off to do a little freelance work of some historical importance before joining Fiat to work on gas turbines and eventually emerge as boss of Fiat's automotive engines division.

Ferrari, as we have said, is a proud man. He does not like to appear a failure, and he often seems reluctant to admit that anyone else might do better. It takes little imagination to see what would have happened to his pride if, after the great damp squib act of 1955, the Ferrari team were to be a tremendous success in 1956 running Lancias. Whether for this reason or

Some of the 1957 F1 Ferrari cars had no side pontoons or fairings, others retained the 1956 shape. One of each crashed by the harbour during the Monaco GP. Schell is passing in Scarlatti's Maserati

because he genuinely believed that Lancia was wrong he set about having Jano's design altered in several respects: most of these were matters of detail but one was fundamental, being aimed at doing away with the pontoon tanks that were the most memorable feature of the D50. Initially he simply removed most of the fuel capacity to the tail of the car, though he made it plain from the outset that he intended to get rid of the side tanks altogether as soon as he could. This could not all be done at once, and to cover himself against criticism from the people who were supporting him financially it would not be desirable for it all to be done at once.

So he began the 1956 season, in the Argentine, with a motley collection. There were the standard Lancia D50, a Lancia fitted with the rear end of a Super Squalo, a Super Squalo fitted with a Lancia engine, a standard Super Squalo, and a shortened version of the Ferrari with all the fuel tanks removed to the tail.

Ferrari also began the 1956 season with the best Grand Prix driver in the world, for the withdrawal of Daimler-Benz from racing had left Fangio open to offers. Retaining his services bore immediate fruit, for Fangio won both the Argentine and Mendoza Grands Prix; but it must have impaired Ferrari's sense of achievement that the master driver was successful in a car that owed far more to Jano than to Lampredi. The more modified cars were clearly inferior, and handled abysmally.

When the European season opened at Syracuse, Fangio made fastest practice lap in a new version of the Lancia-Ferrari in which the gap between the pontoons and the central fuselage had been filled to give the effect of a full-width body within the wheelbase. These pontoons were now empty of fuel, a pair of small tanks being placed on each side of the cockpit while the bulk of the fuel was in the tail of the car. In one respect at least there was a distinct improvement: the rudimentary and inefficient exhaust system of the

By 1958 the Ferrari was again wholly Ferrari, with a new V6 engine. This was the Dino, driven here by Hawthorn to win the French GP and lapping the Maserati of P Hill. Very sportingly Hawthorn declined to lap Fangio who finished fourth Lancia had given way to a bulky but uncoupled type, each cylinder having its own separate pipe, so that there were clusters of four sweeping through the pontoons and terminating in short megaphones just ahead of the rear wheels.

pendent swing-axle rear suspension, which proved in practice to have been a ghastly mistake. Still, progress was being made; and by June 1956, Fangio was able to put in an exceptionally fast practice lap at Spa for the Belgian GP. Being somewhat put out by a very quick lap by Moss in a Maserati in 4min 14.7 sec., Fangio tried hard and reduced this to 4min 9.8. This was 8.8 seconds faster than he had managed the previous year when driving the Mercedes-Benz, and 8.3 seconds faster than Castelotti had achieved on the same occasion in the original Lancia D50. The times are not strictly comparable, for the circuit had been cleaned up slightly, but it is improbable that this could account for more than half of the improvement, leaving an increase of lap speed of perhaps two per cent to be credited either to development of the Lancia or to the driving prowess of Fangio. In fact the Maserati was faster on the straight than the Lancia-Ferrari, which was geared to do about 165mph at 8200 rpm; and the Vanwall was at least another ten miles an hour faster. Despite this, first and second place at the end of the race went to Ferrari.

It was definitely Ferrari's year for winning races. Not until the Italian GP did the team come unstuck, all but one of the cars succumbing to tyre failures, the usual symptom being tread separation as the cars were driven around the Monza bankings. The one car which did not thus suffer was Fangio's, and his went out with steering failure, like the car crashed in practice by von Trips. But despite this setback Fangio was the year's world champion driver, and the Ferrari was still the car to beat.

There was even some reason to suppose that the final definitive form of the car had been reached, for by the time of the German GP in August all the five team cars were identical. Yet when 1957 brought its first frolics in Argentina there were changes to be seen again. In fact they were hardly the same cars. The chassis and suspension were new; and so was the engine, designed

As the season wore on, changes continued. Detail alterations to the rear suspension and chassis structure were numerous, the different versions of oil cooler type and location were innumerable. At Naples there was even an experimental version with fully inde-

by Bellantani and Bazzi as a V8 again but otherwise more like a Ferrari than its predecessor. Where the Lancia engine had finger tappets, hairpin valve springs, and a barrel-like crankcase, the new Ferrari V8 had mushroom tappets, coil springs, and a boxy crankcase. Its bore was greater, its stroke less, its peak revs higher (8600 rpm at which the engine was reputed to deliver 260bhp). But on this basis its bmep at maximum power was the same as before, a modest 159lb/in^2. According to the drivers, it was a slower car than the Lancia – and Ferrari no longer had Fangio by way of compensation, for he had moved to Maserati.

Various minor races came and went until at the end of April 1957 the travelling circus came to Naples – and brought with it a new Formula 2 Ferrari. Its chassis was not particularly noteworthy – what Ferrari's ever is ? – but Bellantani had done a conventionally competent job on it. The engine was something quite new though, a Jano-designed V6 — not half of an existing V12 (which might have been a convenient way of encompassing a 1½ litre capacity) but an entirely new design with two slightly staggered cylinder blocks separated by a most peculiar included angle of 65 degrees. 120 degrees would have been perfectly all right, and 60 might have seemed reasonable ; yet the best of an unconvincing bunch of explanations for this peculiar 65 degree interval was that it gave enough room for the twin overhead camshafts on each cylinder bank. I am not convinced but that does not matter ; the facts are that the engine worked, that such imbalance as it suffered was not significant, and that it ushered in a new generation of V6 Ferrari engines which in all their confusing multiplicity were to bring as much honour and glory to the name as anything that Ferrari ever put into a Grande Epreuve.

It was Ferrari's son Dino, to whom the old man was devoted, who suggested the idea of a V6, and the engine and car were named after him. So were to be many subsequent V6s, and it is worth a little diversion to clarify the pattern. This first one, which appeared as a 1.5-litre engine at Naples, had two overhead camshafts to each flank, dual ignition (the twelve plugs were fed by a pair of magnetos driven off the noses of the inlet camshafts) and dry-sump lubrication. Jano designed it with assistance from Franco Rocchi, and he laid out two basic cylinder blocks, one allowing up to 2 litres swept volume and the other up to 3 litres. This Dino engine was used in Formula 2 and Formula 1 and in sports cars run by the factory team. In the early 1960s there was a 120 degree V6 also called the Dino – as was a V8, which was designed by Chiti.

Next, demonstrating the high-speed engine-building virtuosity which is Ferrari's forte, came another V6, this time set at 60 degrees and with a single camshaft in each cylinder head. This was essentially a cut-price Dino for sale to the public, though it has seen its way into a Grand Prix car.

Later came another 65 degree V6. This one was wholly the work of Rocchi, a design intended to lend itself to quantity production by Fiat so that it might satisfy homologation requirements for Formula 2 racing in the 1960s. It has been through a number of changes over the years, and we shall come to them in due time and place ; but let us return to 1957 and Naples.

The fact that it was 1957 is important. It was known then that in the following year Grand Prix cars would have to run on petrol rather than on the heady confections of alcohol, benzole, nitromethane and acetone that had made Grand Prix racing such a delightfully smelly business. One of the most significant features of the Dino engine was that it had been designed to be suitable for petrol, thus giving Ferrari a head start for the future. With its head still arranged to give a compression

Hawthorn talking to John Bolster (back to camera) with three Dini lined up at the pits

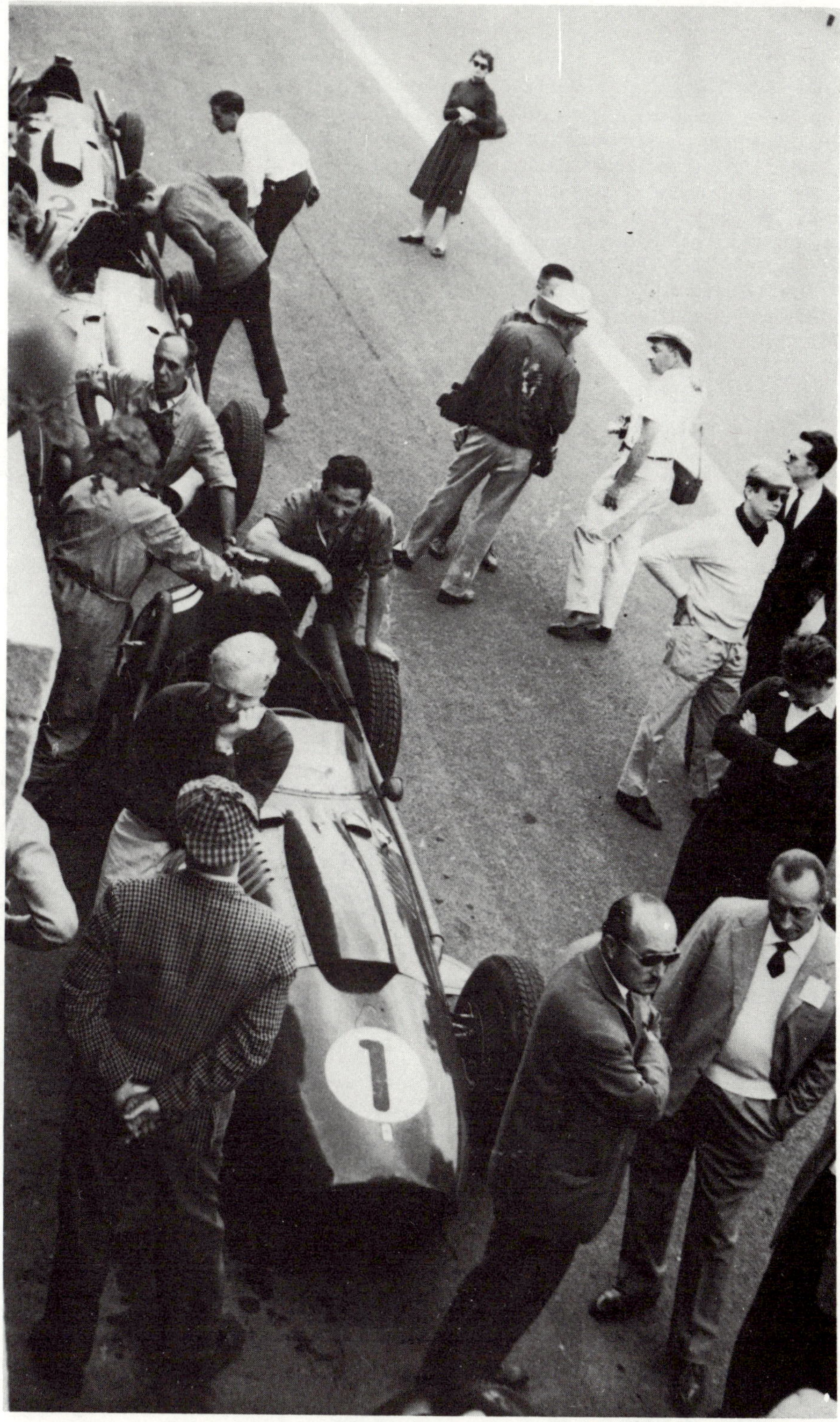

ratio of 9½:1, this 1½-litre engine was reputed to yield 190bhp at 9200 rpm. The estimate may have been justified, for in practice Musso completed a lap in the 1½-litre car only 1.7 seconds slower than the new record established by Hawthorn in the 2½-litre V8 car.

The V8 was still going, but not so well; and in events of greater status, when it came up against doughtier opposition, it was no longer very competitive. The Maseratis were appreciably faster now, allowing Fangio to become world champion yet again; and the Vanwalls wanted only a little reliability to outstrip the lot.

In 1958, they got it; but by that time the Ferrari V8 was effectively and officially finished. In a process of experiment and enlargement that took it to the Modena GP with 1.86 litres inside it, and to the Moroccan GP with 2.4 litres, the Dino V6 had grown up into a very fast and quite compact little Formula 1 car, to be the mainstay of the team for the next three years. With a bore and stroke of 85 and 71 millimetres respectively, it was safe to 9400 rpm although the recommended limit was 8500 and the peak power output (280bhp) was realised at 8300. It had its successes, but they were not frequent. In 1958 the Vanwall was virtually supreme, and in the following two years the revolution inspired by Cooper and abetted by Lotus, whereby the design and morphology of the racing car was completely revised to

The Dino looked bulbous from behind but was lighter and more compact than its predecessors, as might befit its F2 origins

put the engine behind the driver, caused new standards of performance, and especially of handling and cornering ability, to be set. They were standards which the classical front-engined Ferrari was simply unable to match. As its career drew to a close it acquired independent rear suspension in place of its de Dion axle, but this did not enable it to keep up with Cooper or Lotus on a twisting circuit. By 1960 its only hope of success was on circuits such as the Avus in Berlin where handling was at a discount and high power and speed were at a premium.

Another shortcoming from which the Dino suffered in 1958 was weak brakes. By this time most of its opponents were making good use of discs, though it is fair to say that at the beginning of the season they suffered more problems with them than Ferrari did with drums. Nevertheless, while they worked discs were demonstrably better and one would have thought that this had been demonstrated to Ferrari quite convincingly at Le Mans some time earlier. But Ferrari has a marked distaste for copying or even appearing to copy others. Apparently he also disliked the idea of obtaining components from Britain: and at that time Britain was almost the only source of good disc brakes, although the Vanwall had consistently satisfactory results from a Goodyear design. So Ferrari tried to make a disc brake of his own, and to make it different from existing ones.

The brake was an abject failure, and the old man had eventually to admit defeat. This was brought about by degrees, beginning with the privately commissioned modification of a road-going 250 GT Ferrari used by Peter Collins for transport. After Collins was killed at the Nurburgring, Hawthorn arranged for these Dunlop brakes to be removed and fitted to his racing car. The modification meant that the wire-spoked wheels had to be rebuilt in order to give clearance for the brake calipers. This was done in time for the Italian GP at the end of the 1958 season where once again the Ferrari team, using Englebert tyres whose qualities of endurance seemed still to leave something to be desired, had tyre trouble. There was a Ferrari on the front row of the starting grid, having proved third fastest in practice, and this marked a further aggrandizement of the Dino engine, the stroke of which had been lengthened by a millimetre to raise the capacity to 2451cc. Now that it was nearer 2.5 litres than 2.4, its title (following the new system of engine designation recently introduced by Ferrari) became Dino 256 – a figure upon which Ferrari could not improve when means were found for making the swept volume 2470cc in time for the 1959 season. But it did him no good: never again would the manufacturers' championship or the drivers' championship be won in a front-engined racing car.

71

THE REAR ENGINED SINGLE SEATERS

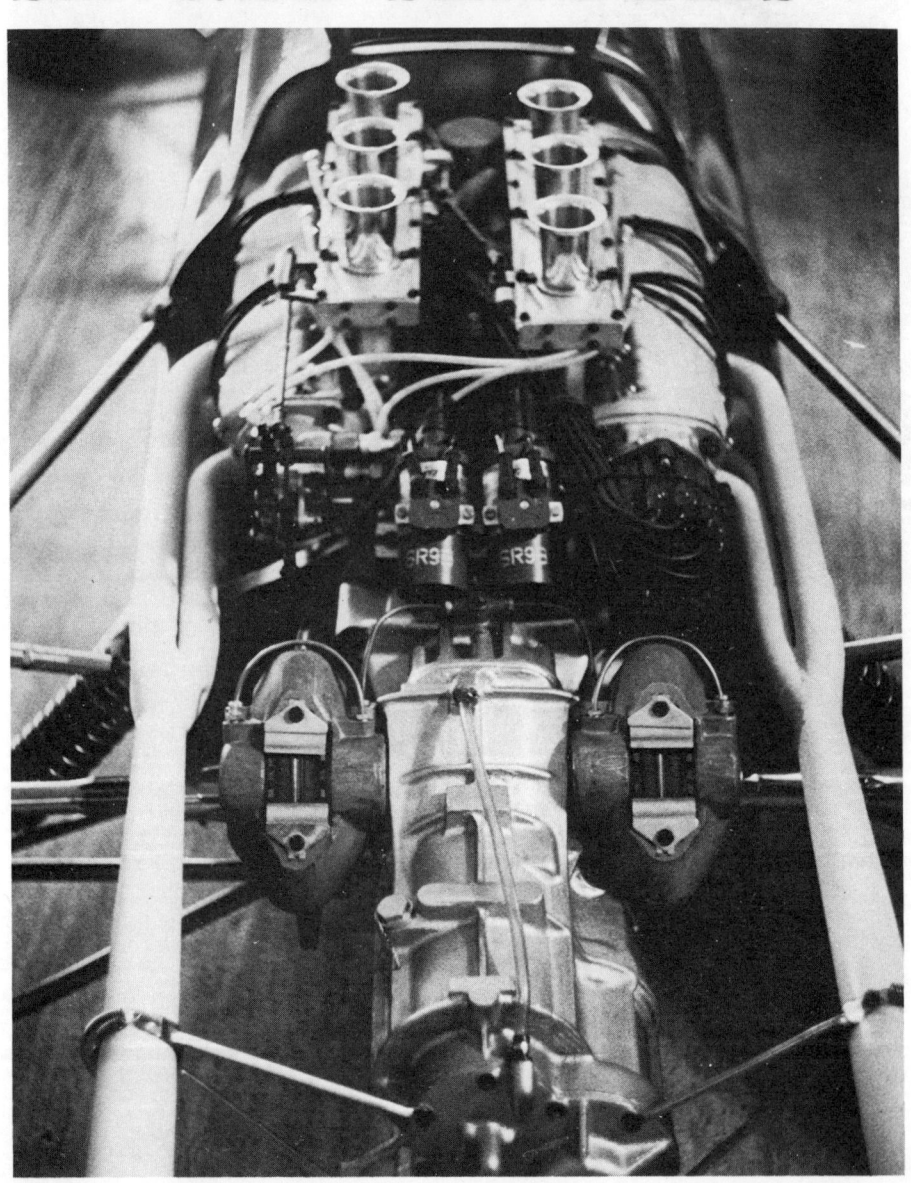

When the first classic of the 1959 GP season started at Monaco in May, seven of the sixteen starters were rear-engined. Two years later all would be rear-engined; and this was anticipated by Ferrari in 1960 when he fielded a rear-engined Grand Prix car for the first time at Monaco.

It was just one third of a second slower than the best of the front-engined Ferraris in practice. The front engined car was two seconds slower than the Lotus 18 in which Moss took pole position and won the race comfortably.

Reluctantly Ferrari eventually agreed to the idea to putting the driver before the engine. Stubborn to the last, he carried on as though his motto was taken from Dr Johnson: 'No man, sir, was ever great by imitation'. So the locals at Modena must have been taken aback one morning when a rear-engined Ferrari turned up at the track with the factory's chief tester, Severi, driving it. Before long he took it back, reporting sorrowfully that when he put the accelerator down the front wheels came up. Presumably something suitable was done to the weight distribution and suspension geometry for this was the car that went to Monaco to show the world how open-minded and free from prejudice Ferrari was. It was entered as a 2.1-litre affair but was really a full 2½ litres, the subterfuge being intended to provide a measure of face-saving in the event of the car being a hopeless failure. In a sense it was a failure anyway, for Ferrari decided that no further development work should be done on it. He decided instead to concentrate on getting a new rear-engined 1½-litre car ready for the new formula in 1961.

It was not to be a particularly original piece of design, especially the chassis.

This F2 Ferrari engine was never seriously raced, but served as a design study for a new 4-valve cylinder head closely-paired overhead camshafts which proved very fast in the F1 races of 1968

Most of the inspiration for it came from the Cooper which Ferrari obtained from the *Scuderia Centro-Sud* who had raced it unsuccessfully with a Maserati engine. But a Cooper chassis is a Cooper chassis whatever engine you stick in it, and the sight of Brabham, McLaren and Moss riding roughshod over all his precious Dinos had presumably impressed upon Ferrari the notion that the Cooper was the ideal according to which all rear-engined cars should be built. In this he was of course wrong, for the Coopers achieved good results for reasons which had nothing to do with their hacksaw-and-welding-torch approach to the gentle art of tubular frame design.

At any rate it was hardly surprising that the rear-engined Ferrari was, to put it politely, derivative in its design. Nobody expected it to be superior to the British cars in the chassis department. On the other hand everybody knew that none of the British cars would have a respectable engine, whereas Ferrari could be relied upon to produce something new, reliable and far more powerful than anything his opposition might field. By now the job of maintaining this reputation had been given to engineer Chiti, and he set about modifying both the prototype chassis and the 1½-litre V6 engine.

The car was ready for the Syracuse GP, which as usual came very early in the European season. In its new 73×58.8 mm form the engine gave about 180 bhp at up to 9000 rpm. The chassis was basically similar to the 1960 Formula 2 and had a great deal in common with that of the Cooper. Its tubes were of a fairly large diameter, full of kinks and curves which permitted bending stresses and provided a negation of everything that space-frame theory stipulates. Suspension was by double wishbones fore and aft, while the whole car was very narrow tracked and low. A clever transmission layout helped the low shape and more importantly helped to keep the clutch cool. There had been lots of failures in the earlier V8s and Dinos, where the clutch was

73

Above: When at last Ferrari built a rear-engined GP car, it was the fastest thing in 1961—because of its engine rather than its chassis. Here is the late Ricardo Rodriguez in the version with 120° engine. Below: The last Ferrari driver to be the World Champion was John Surtees in 1964, driving the V8 and flat-12 cars. The flat-12, shown here, was out classed in the following year by BRM and Lotus

conventionally located behind the engine. While all other constructors placed the clutch immediately behind the engine and ahead of the final drive housing, Ferrari placed his at the extreme tail of the car, driven by a quill shaft that passed through the gearbox. At its other extremity the car was equally distinguished: instead of the simple Pitot nose such as on the British cars, the Ferrari sported a rakish pair of nostril-like intakes for the radiator air. This was a Chiti trademark, looking like mere styling but which had proved in Ferrari's wind tunnel to improve the aerodynamic penetration of the nose.

The Italian car could be distinguished from all those new-fangled British ones in yet another respect. Everyone was using cast alloy wheels except Ferrari, who maintained some link with past glories by old-fashioned centre-lock wire wheels. These were at last shod with Dunlop tyres, set at rather extreme angles of negative camber which looked very dramatic and caused no end of trouble with high tread temperatures.

Despite all this, or because of it, the Ferrari won at Syracuse, even though it was chased furiously by the factory Porsche. Yet it was just an interim design, for at the next race there was a new V6 Ferrari with its cylinder banks set at the more accommodating angle of 120 degrees. This new engine, which appeared at Monaco, was fitted into a chassis of the same type as that already seen at Syracuse. Chiti's new engine was expected to rev at higher speeds because of the smoother running of a 120 degree V6. It was clearly very powerful, and Ginther made second fastest practice lap. It was significant that he was sandwiched on the front row of the grid between the brilliant new Lotus of Clark and the older Lotus 18 of Moss who was faster than Ginther by 0.2 per cent. During the race both these drivers improved enormously on their practice lap speeds. The pace was absolutely furious and Moss completed one of the three greatest drives of his distinguished career. His Lotus, like all the British cars, gave away 25bhp to the Ferrari, but partly made up for it by smaller frontal area, lighter weight, greater cornering power and better braking. But it was not the car which won the race, it was the driver. Moss led Ginther home by just 3.6 seconds after two and three-quarter hours racing.

He beat Ginther again by an even narrower margin at Zandvoort, but ahead of the two of them was Clark in the newer Lotus, and ahead of him were two Ferraris. If the lower powered but faster cornering British cars could barely hold the Italians at a medium-pace circuit such as the Dutch venue, they could clearly entertain no hopes of being competitive on faster roads. At Spa there were three 120 degree Ferraris on the front row of the grid, the fastest of them being 2.8 per cent faster than the best Cooper, 3.4 per cent faster than the BRM, and 4 per cent faster than the Lotus 18 of Moss. This was not achieved without some chassis tuning: at Dunlop's urgent representation the excess negative camber was reduced, whereupon it was found that the handling of the cars improved and the speed rose while the critical temperatures at the inner edges of the tyre treads were reduced.

For the rest of the season the Ferraris were clearly the fastest cars being fielded, though they did not always win. The German GP was won by Moss in another of his most outstanding races, when with the aid of rain tyres he outcornered the whole field to win, despite a meteoric record lap achieved

Above: Engines grew to 3 litres for the 1966 Grand Prix, and the fastest car (though not the most successful) was the Ferrari. Bandini takes the Hunze Rug hairpin at Zandvoort during the Dutch GP Right: Beginning the 1966 season on Dunlop tyres, Ferrari ended firmly wedded to Firestone, but not before trying Goodyear as well. Details at the tail of the Firestone-shod car (below) include the high-pressure fuel pump surrounded by a protective tubular cage

in pursuit by P Hill. Before the season was over Hill was to emerge as champion driver and Ferrari as champion manufacturer.

Ferrari must have been very proud: and he promptly fell. 1962 was a very bad year for him in Grand Prix racing. It must have been a matter of some surprise to him that the British manufacturers should have come up with some good V8 engines, and since their chassis were already superior to his there was very little that his team could

76

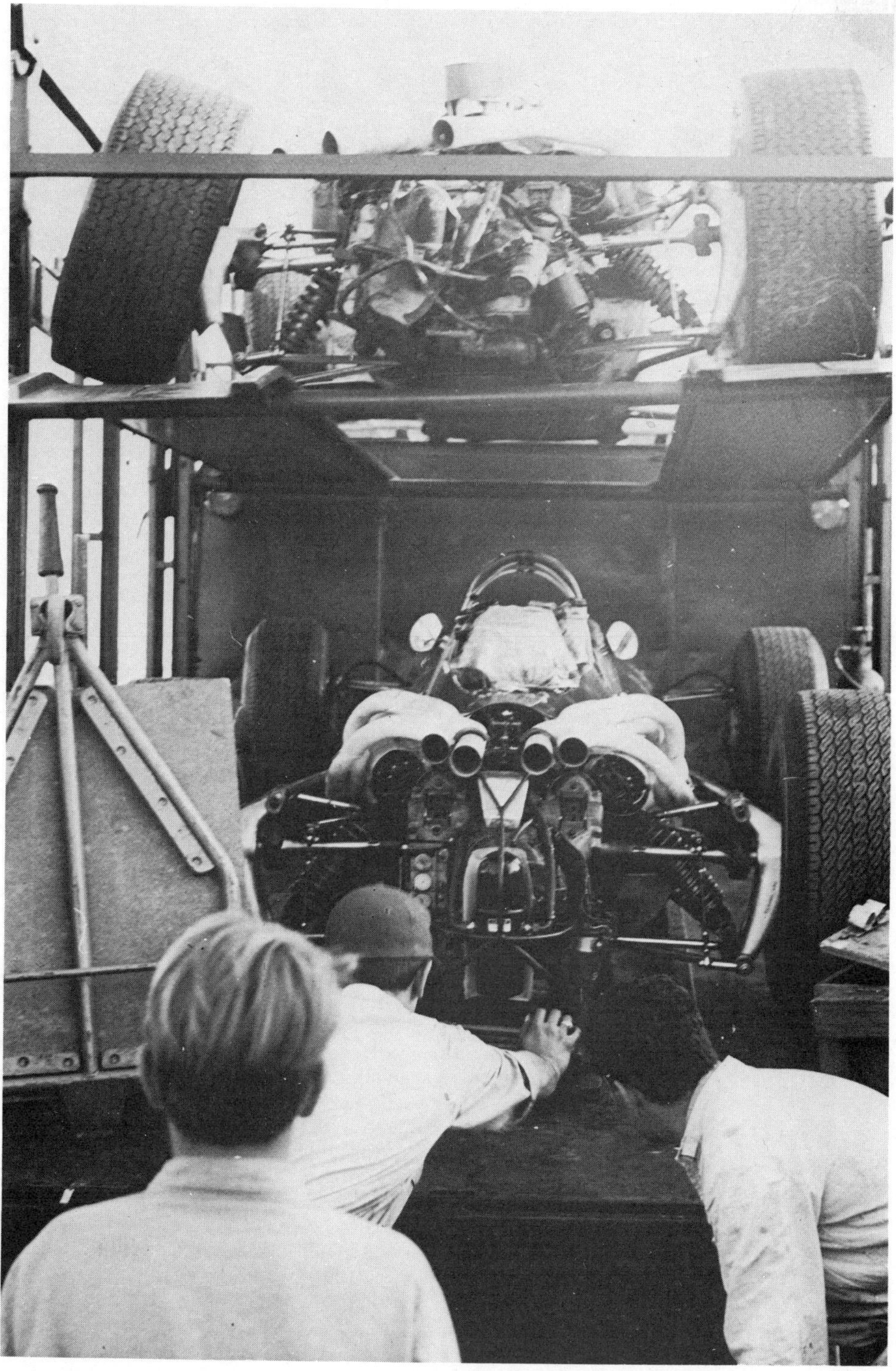

John Surtees with Ferrari

Jackie Ickx

do about it. A revised version of the 120 degree Ferrari appeared at the German GP, the most noticeable difference being that the gearbox was now ahead of the final drive instead of behind it; but this and the six-speed gearbox, together with some cleaning up and simplification of the chassis and suspension, were not enough to bring it up to date. 1962 saw the introduction of the stressed-skin-hull Lotus 25, which was about as big a disaster as Ferrari could expect to face. It also saw the flaming row between the old man and Chiti, culminating in the latter walking out to try his fortune with the ill-fated ATS concern. At the end of the year Ferrari wrote to his drivers Baghetti, Bandini, P Hill and Rodriguez:

'The present position once again makes it impossible for us to carry out plans established since Monza to construct four new Formula 1 cars.'

'Due to the lack of indispensable collaboration by our workmen, reasons that have their origin in a national problem and not one which originates

Team manager Franco Lini with driver Chris Amon in the pits at Brands Hatch in 1968

in our own organisation, we see ourselves forced to renounce future races.'

'We will continue within the limits of the reduced timetable to work on the development of the prototype Formula 1 car in the hope that we will be able to make use of the experience in the future. The above has been communicated to you in the case that you should desire to find other means to compete in the remaining races. . . .'

'We thank you for your collaboration during the present racing season and regret that in the field of Formula 1 we were not able to produce means to compare with our construction for Gran Turismo, sports and prototypes. With my best wishes.'

In fact, little of this may have been sincere. Ferrari was planning to alter the system of driver contracts, concluding that it would be much better for his drivers to be full-time employees of the company who could test drive when they were not racing, rather than part-timers, dilettanti and freelance soldiers of fortune. He certainly got himself an interesting threesome. Mike Parkes was a splendid engineer and a handy driver, particularly useful for the long distance sports car races which were so important to Ferrari. Mairesse, alias Fiery Willy, was all that his nickname implied, and John Surtees was a brilliant driver, a master of track craft, and already immensely popular in Italy as a result of his dazzling succession of world championships won on Italian MV Agusta motor cycles.

The car they had to drive was a joint effort by Jano and Rocchi, and was fashioned after the manner of the all-conquering Lotus. As the year wore on it was further developed with the aid of the brilliant and likeable young Mauro Forghieri. Light alloy wheels, Bosch fuel injection and a new version of the 120 degree V6 engine all made the car progressively more competitive and justified the effort that Surtees was successfully putting into his driving. A 24-valve version of the engine was known to be on its way, but in the meantime

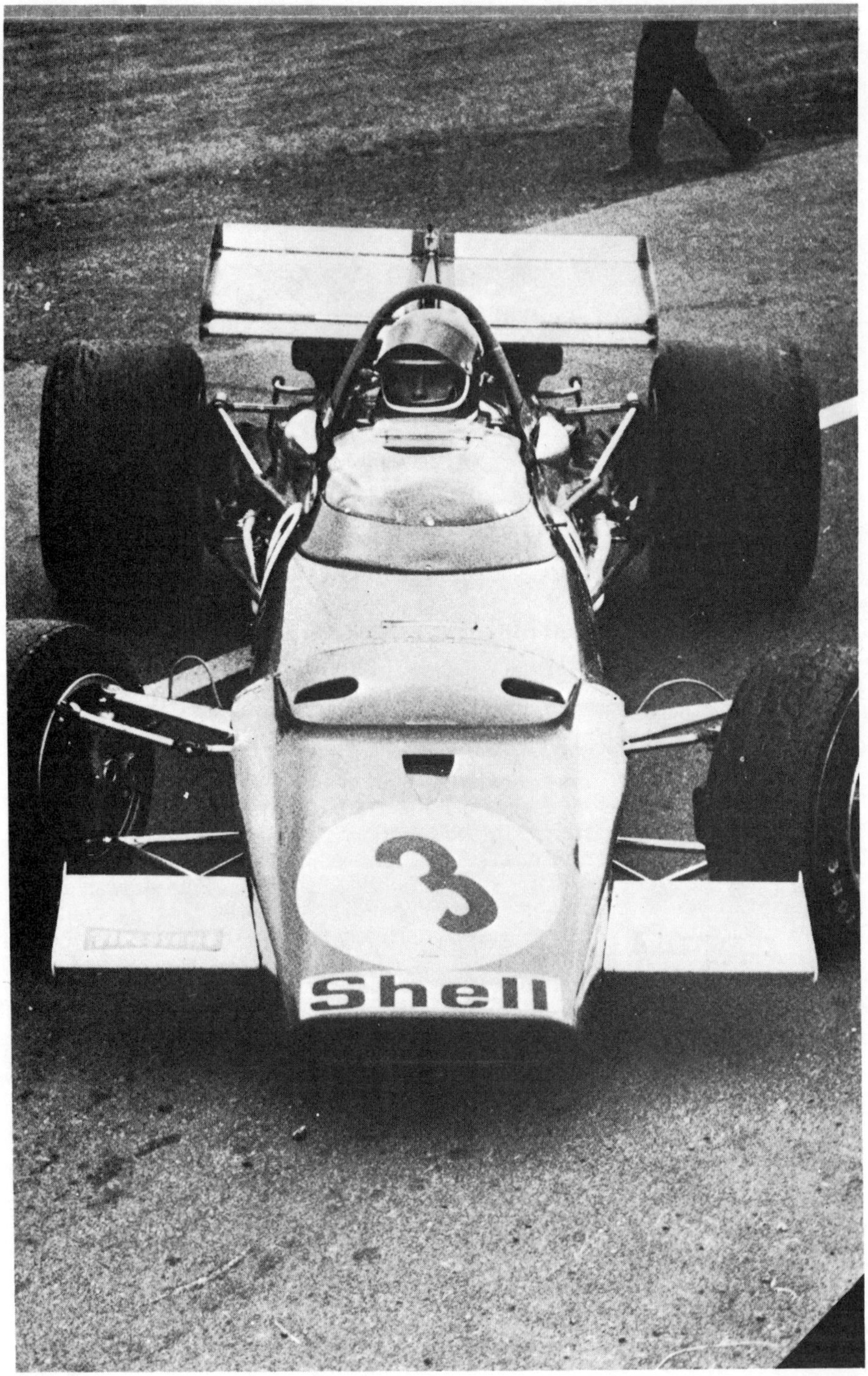
3
Shell

The fastest F1 car at the end of the 1970 season was the flat-12 Ferrari the design of which was the work of Forghieri. Ickx drove this one at the British GP

the existing one had been altered to suit a new chassis, one which marked the abandonment by Ferrari of nearly all his old-fashioned ideas.

The engine was bolted directly onto the bulkhead behind the driver so that it took all lateral and vertical loads from the upper links and lower reversed wishbone of the rear suspension. Tractive and braking forces were transmitted by trailing pairs of radius rods which also picked up at points near the periphery of the bulkhead. Indeed from the bulkhead aft the new Ferrari was very similar to its new contemporary the BRM. Ahead of the bulkhead the structure was almost pure Lotus, with two large longitudinal torsional boxes on each side of the cockpit, linked by a stressed floor and an assortment of double or partial bulkheads. This car led the field at Monza, and indeed ran away from everything except Clark's Lotus until the Ferrari suffered a broken valve and was out of the race. The Lotus kept going and Clark became world champion. Already it was generally accepted that he was an exceptional driver, and the fact that Surtees so often ran him close was ample tribute to the new Ferrari as well as to its driver.

In the following year, 1964, Surtees and Ferrari reigned supreme. He had a new car, the type 158, more than ever like a Lotus but possibly even stiffer for its two pontoons (which provided most of its strength) were rather deeper than those of the English car. Within them were rubber bag fuel tanks, a departure from Ferrari's practice with the V6 where the driver's seat was actually the aluminium petrol tank. Minor changes had been made to the suspension, mainly to suit the new Dunlop racing tyres which were now suitable for thirteen-inch wheels instead of requiring wheels two inches larger in diameter. The Ferrari wore these tyres in a nominal six-inch size at the front and seven-inch at the rear, the latter rims being about nine inches wide.

It is here in 1964 that we may observe the beginnings in Europe of the trend towards wide low-profile tyres, which has continued ever since. These tyres mounted on very wide rims give the utmost traction and stability; but they were not peculiar to Ferrari. The other manufacturers also followed the trend. It was its power output that made the Type 158 superior. Chiti's V8 began with at least 200bhp – 5 more than the Coventry Climax and 10 more than the wide-angle V6 Ferrari – and before long it was giving 215 at 11000 rpm.

The Ferrari V8 was less extreme in its proportions than either of these other engines: its piston area was virtually the same as that of the Coventry Climax, but its ratio of stroke: bore was nearer unity than in either of the others. Thus the mean piston speed of the Ferrari V8 at the peak of the power curve was 3800 feet per minute, more than the others reached but still lower than the 4000 feet per minute generally considered as an acceptable figure in racing engines. In fact, because of its ability to run at higher rates of revolution the Ferrari yielded more power than the British engine, which had deliberately minimised inlet ports so that it got out of breath beyond 9800 rpm.

Only towards the end of this very successful season were more powerful engines to be seen. These newcomers were both 12 cylinder designs. One was the V12 Honda, packed full of roller bearings and set with its crankshaft athwartships. The other was the flat 12 Ferrari which appeared in practice for the Italian GP at Monza and went very well indeed.

The flat 12 had its first race at Watkins Glen in the United States in October, where the field seemed very well matched: fastest of all was Clark's Lotus, and just three per cent slower was the Honda – but between these two

81

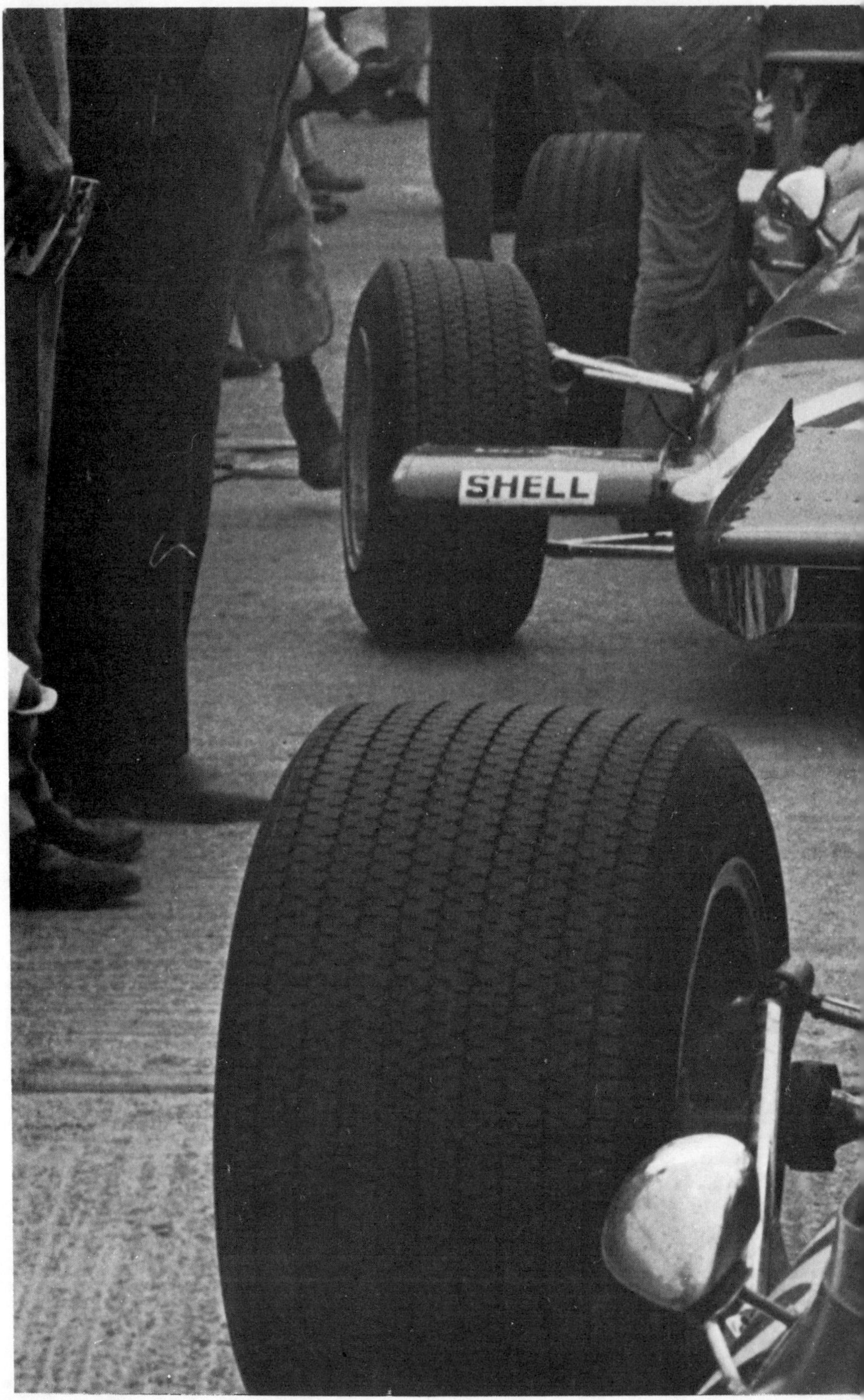
SHELL

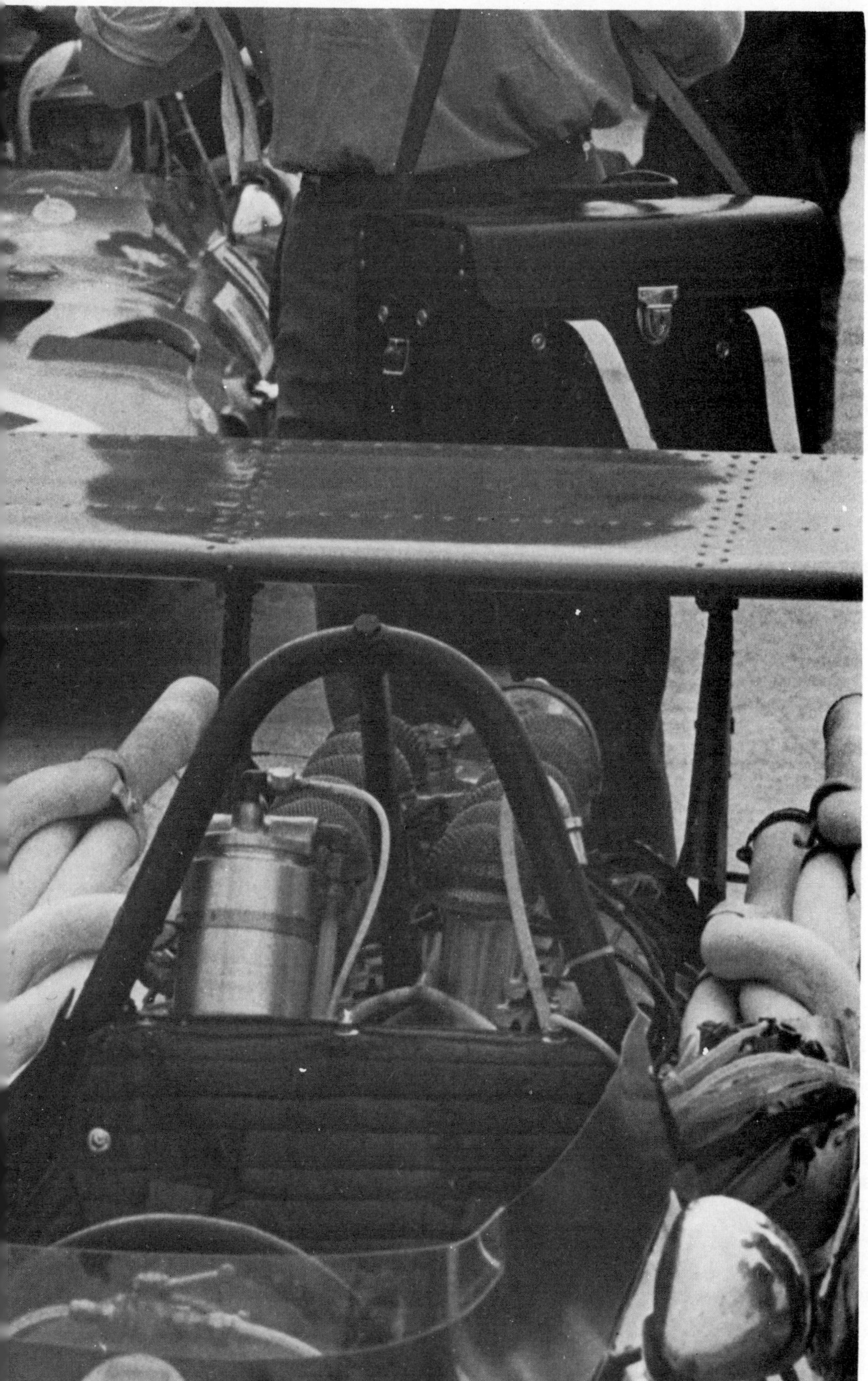

were twelve other cars, of which the best was the Ferrari V8 and by no means the worst the Ferrari flat 12. By the time of the Mexican GP, however, the flat 12 was proving the faster of the two Ferrari designs. But despite this, team manager Dragoni continued to assign it to Bandini, leaving the premier driver, Surtees, with the V8. Bandini was undoubtedly very fast, but there was equally no doubt that Surtees was faster and considerably more experienced, and on such occasions as at Monaco in 1965 it was patent that there was a great deal of rivalry between them. There was also considerable friction between the Ferrari organisation and Surtees who, whatever his advantages in skill and experience, suffered the disadvantage of being honest, forthright and intolerant of anything less than 100 per cent effort by those working with him, and most of all the inestimable disadvantage of not being Italian.

The original idea behind fielding the two alternative engines was that the V8 should be used on relatively slow circuits and the flat 12 on the faster ones, two examples of each being planned early in 1964. It has been said that the flat 12 was merely the old Colombo-designed 1½ litre V12 cut in two and spread out a bit. This is a facile dismissal of a considerable undertaking, equivalent to describing the albatross as a mere adaption of the primeval archeopteryx. It is true that the bore and stroke of the flat 12 were the same as those of the original supercharged V12, but these were soon revised to increase the piston area, and with these later dimensions the flat 12 was reputed to develop 225bhp, only five more than was attributed to the V8. Yet the flat 12 had 14 per cent more piston area than the V8; and since it could also rev faster without reaching the same mean piston velocity, it should have been considerably more powerful than the V8, not just a little more.

From this it can be deduced that the mean effective pressure in its cylinders was lower, with which observation is usually associated a flatter torque curve. Thus while giving only slightly more power, the flat 12 may have had a wider spread of torque and therefore been easier to drive and to exploit than the V8. Certainly the intakes of the flat 12 were less favourably shaped for the best possible breathing, though this was rectified in a developed version of the engine which appeared at Monza in 1965. By this time a new cylinder head had been designed, having the inlet ports entering the combustion chambers at a different angle so that the long intake rampipes sloped slightly outwards instead of being vertical as previously.

Unfortunately for Ferrari, Coventry Climax had been working in an even more inspired fashion on their existing V8, whose new cylinder heads with four valves to each combustion chamber gave it such performance that Clark's Lotus was almost invincible. Indeed the Italian GP at the end of the European season was the first race in the championship series that Clark's type 33 Lotus had lost since the Monaco GP at the beginning of that season. It is possible, given time and the attentions of Franco Rocchi who was becoming established as a man of great importance in Ferrari engine design and development, that the flat 12 might eventually have acquired sufficient superiority as a car to counter the unquestioned superiority of Clark as a driver. But there was not time: once again the period of validity of a Grand Prix formula was expiring with Ferrari vanquished.

The terms of the new Formula 1 for Grand Prix racing, due to come into effect at the beginning of 1966, were announced by the FIA in December 1963. The manufacturers therefore had two years in which to prepare themselves; but as is so often the case, their first efforts under the new Formula were very tentative. Pundits were forecasting all sorts of outlandish develments for the future, talking glibly of engines developing 500 bhp and requiring four-wheel-drive in order to exploit them; but in 1966 nobody expected to see anything significantly different from what had just been seen, except that it would be bigger. The 1½-litre formula did not remain in effect for long, and therefore the cars racing at its end were little more than developed versions of those envisaged at its beginning. This excused the similarity to them of the cars which raced in 1966, a similarity which could be seen as much in the new Ferrari as in the other makes.

Of these others several were having to adapt cars that had originally been constructed with the Tasman formula in mind. They were essentially 1½-litre chassis stretched or adapted to accommodate 2½-litre engines. Ferrari had one, virtually a 1965 chassis with a Dino 246 engine in it, and this car ran very well at Syracuse and at Monaco in 1966. Nevertheless it was merely a second string on both occasions for Ferrari was ready at the very beginning of the season with his new 3-litre car.

New was perhaps not the word for it. Bearing in mind Ferrari's astonishing ability to create new engines very rapidly it came as something of a surprise when the new Ferrari proved to have a V12 engine which, superficially at any rate, was very like all the other Colombo-based 3-litre V12s that had been the mainstay of his production for so many years. In fact this 1966 3-litre was a modified version of the 3.3-litre engine used in sports-racing prototypes the year before. As for the chassis, it was essentially similar to the 1965 racers, though somewhat larger in order to accommodate not only the bigger engine but also the bigger quantity of fuel that would be needed to support it. The distance or duration of a race remained unchanged under the new formula, and all the other regulations persisted except that the minimum weight limit was increased from 450 to 500 kilograms.

The greater weight and speed of the new car prompted an increase of wheel diameter to 14 inches, and at the beginning of the season these wheels were shod with Dunlop R7 tyres. Another interesting change from previous Ferrari practice was to place the clutch behind the engine instead of at the tail of the gearbox. But otherwise there was very little to remark about the car except that at Syracuse and at Monaco it was clearly faster than anything else. It failed at Monaco only because its differential broke up in the early stages of the race.

After a surprise defeat by the new Repco-Brabham in a minor event at Silverstone, the V12 Ferrari then proved itself convincingly the fastest car at Spa, where experiments were made with Firestone tyres as an alternative to Dunlop during practice. A difficulty in finding the right combination of wheels and tyres had resulted in poor handling at Silverstone, but now Surtees took the car around Spa in 3 minutes 40.4 seconds on Dunlops, and 3 minutes 38 seconds on Firestones. Race day was wet however, and as no practising had been done with wet-weather Firestone tyres, Surtees chose Dunlops and won the race very convincingly. Incidentally, negotiations for the contractual agreement between Ferrari and Firestone were begun at Monza in 1965 when Ferrari told the tyre company's emissaries that he would be quite happy to race on their tyres provided that they could also produce a tyre of radial-ply construction suitable for all his production cars. They managed eventually, though it was not a task to which they applied themselves with any evident enthusiasm or particular success. On the other hand, the Firestone racing tyres proved most satisfactory on dry circuits, and after some protracted development the American firm also evolved tyres suitable for wetter conditions. Ferrari tried Goodyear as well, doubtless impressed by the outstanding performance of the Repco-Brabham.

All these were matters of perhaps interesting detail, but the car as a whole remained unremarkable by the standards we have come to apply to Ferrari

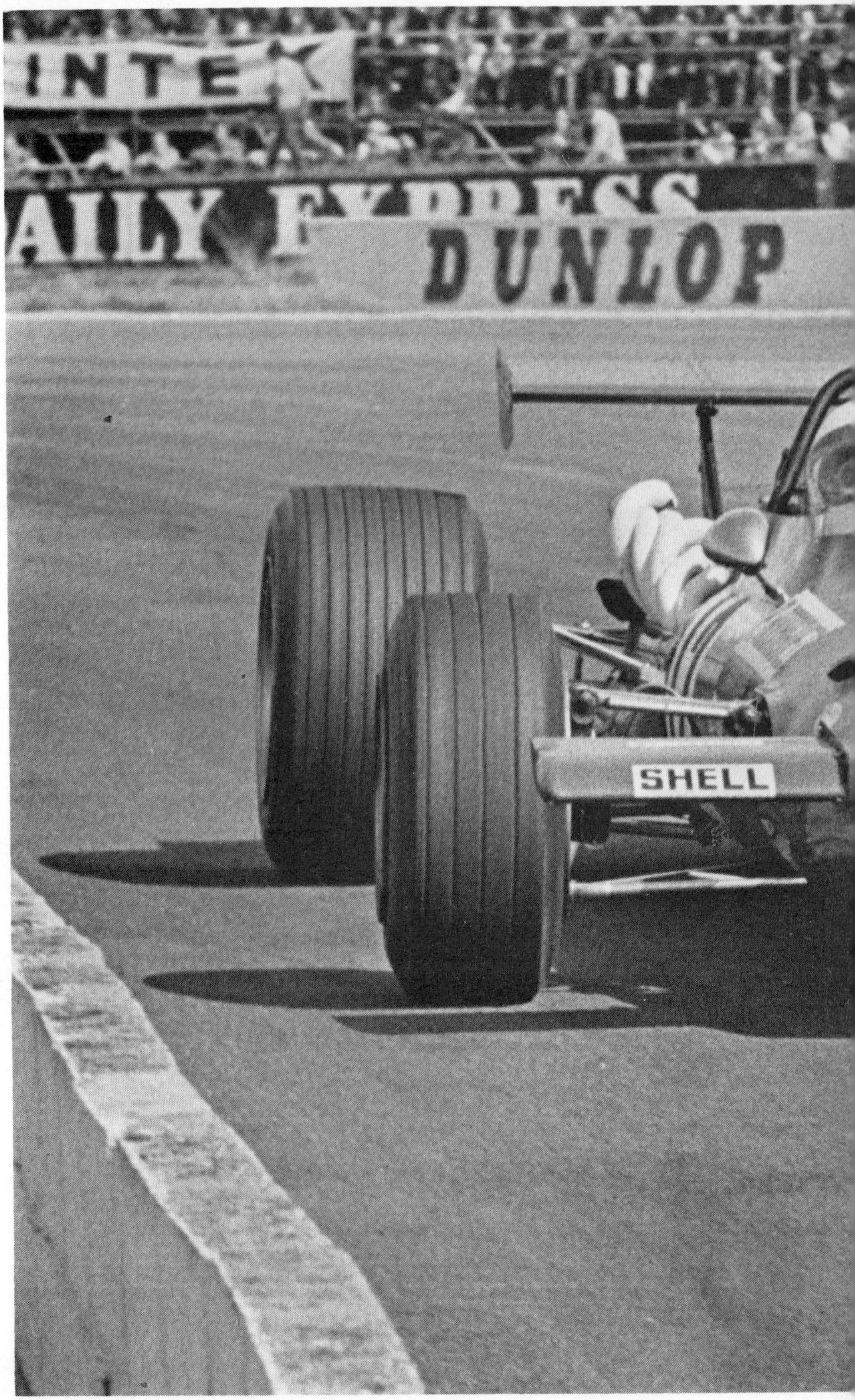
INTE
DUNLOP
SHELL

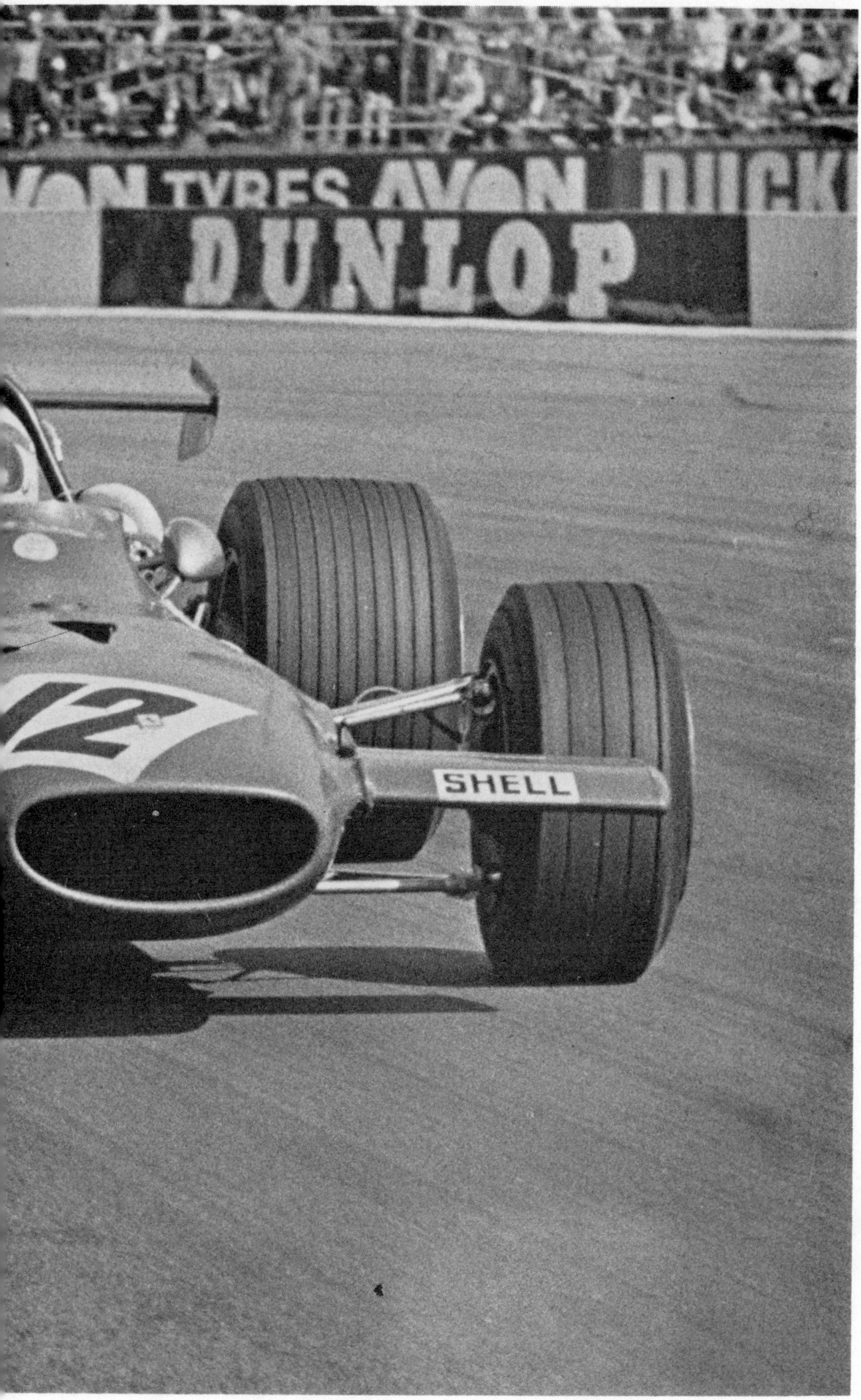
TYRES AVON
DUNLOP
12
SHELL

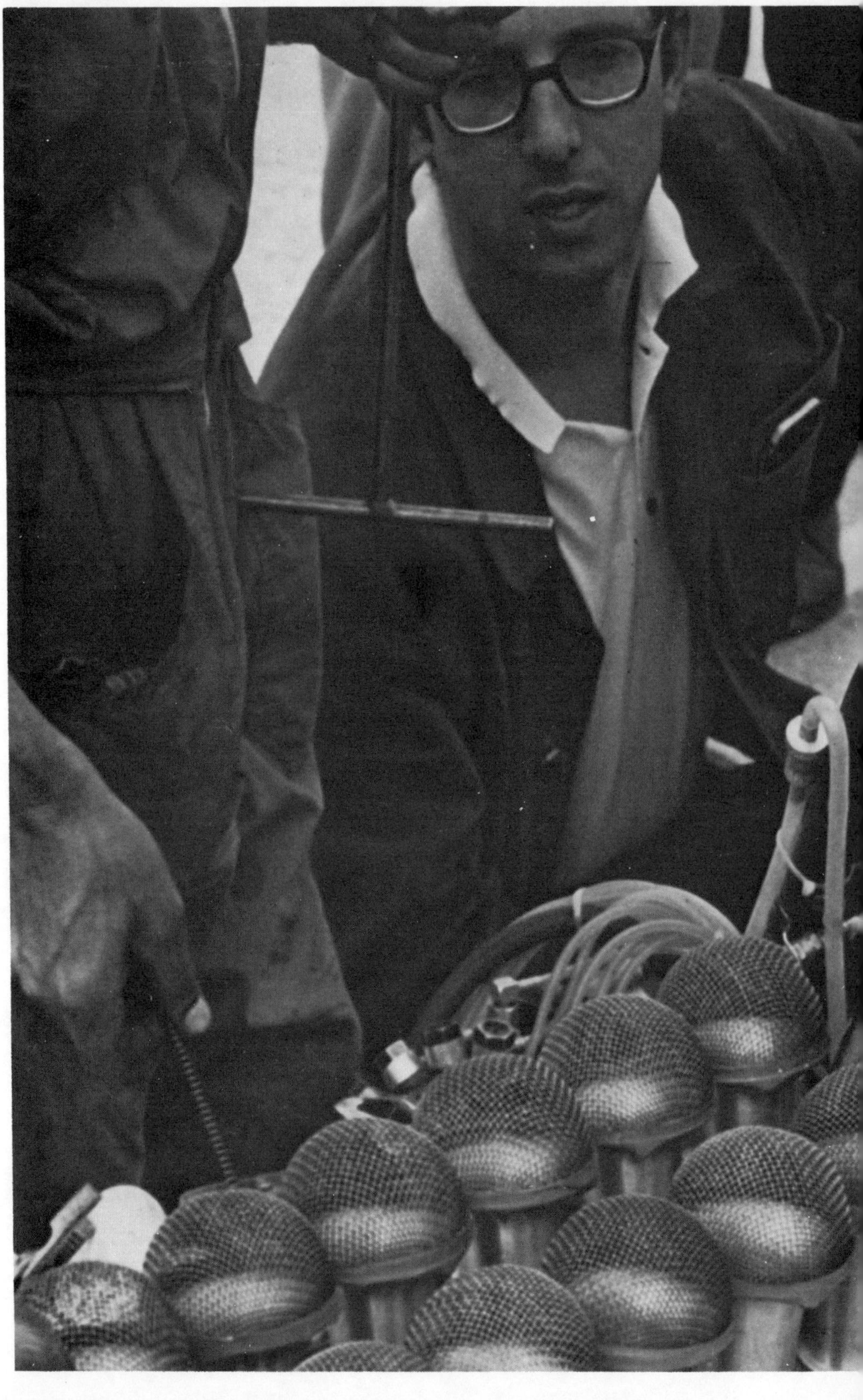

Grand Prix racers. The main frame, compounded of multi-tubular structures and stressed skin, merely echoed previous Ferrari practice, and reflected a 'belt-and-braces' philosophy not encountered among his rivals. The same applied to the suspension, and to the transmission. As a whole the car was larger than those of previous years, as expected; but it compared favourably with the other 3-litre cars which were slowly making their debut. The Repco-Brabham might have been lighter and looked smaller, but in frontal area was virtually identical to the Ferrari. All the other new cars were more bulky and only very late in 1966 could any of the other new engines, such as the V12 Honda and Gurney-Weslake or the horrifyingly badly devised H16 BRM, rival the Ferrari in power and reliability.

In fact the Ferrari was probably the best all-rounder of 1966. On a really slow circuit such as Monaco it had the measure of all its rivals, being bettered in practice only by the formidable combination of Clark and the Lotus 33. On a medium-paced circuit it proved capable of cornering as fast as any of its opposition; and on very fast circuits such as Spa and Reims its speed could not be matched by any other car. This was well demonstrated at Reims when, by slipstreaming the Ferraris, the top speed of the Repco-Brabham rose from 172mph to 185! By September, the date for the Italian GP at Monza, the other manufacturers might be expected to have had cars whose speed on this fast and open track should equal the Ferrari. But this was a time when Ferrari was traditionally expected to pull something new out of the bag for the wildly enthusiastic Italian public. Sure enough the car appeared with a new cylinder head in which each combustion chamber carried three valves instead of two, the two inlets

Mauro Forghieri and the 48-valve Rocchi V12 of the 1969 F1 cars. The earlier 36-valve design could be distinguished by its exhaust pipes in the centre of the V

being supplied by tracts passing between the banks of valves instead of being, as hitherto, virtually a side-draught design. The product of this modification was an increase in power of approximately six per cent, an increase which served to give the Ferrari once more a barely contestable superiority in speed over its rivals.

With these advantages, why was the 1966 Ferrari not a greater success? Why was it that the world championship went to the Repco-Brabham team, whose cars were powered by a very simple engine of disarmingly humble origins? The answer has little to do with the car, for it is simply that at Le Mans in 1966 team manager Dragoni finally pushed Surtees beyond the brink of endurance. Surtees departed and for the rest of the season Ferrari did not have a driver of comparable quality. It has been suggested time and again by authorities and commentators without number that if Ferrari had not alienated Surtees he would undoubtedly have been world champion in 1966. As it was, the best drivers that Ferrari could muster were Parkes and Bandini, the latter admittedly giving a very good account of himself at Watkins Glen and only losing at Reims through breakage of the throttle linkage.

For 1967 Ferrari tried to strengthen his line-up by employing Amon as first-string driver. The young New Zealander was undoubtedly capable of going extremely fast and had the further valuable attribute of being one of the very finest test drivers in the business; but he sometimes seemed to encounter some psychological barrier in overtaking, which left his track craft somewhat inferior to his driving skill. He took quite a long time to play himself in during the opening rounds of the season, but for the rest of the year drove very well and consistently fast to make the best of his car, which was nevertheless overshadowed by the brilliant performance of the new Cosworth-engined Lotus.

Ferrari ended the year in fourth place for the constructor's championship, behind Brabham, behind Lotus and even behind Cooper-Maserati. Amon took fourth place in the driver's listing behind Hulme, Brabham and Clark. Before the end of the year, however, there was promise of better things when a new Ferrari was fielded for the Italian GP in September. It looked sleeker and was in fact lighter, largely due to a new gearbox which was a derivation of a Formula 2 design. The most important feature was a completely new 48-valve engine, the work of Rocchi. Its cylinder heads were reminiscent of a layout previously seen on an experimental Formula 2 car with the twin overhead camshafts set very close together. The cylinder head was so crowded that there was room only for single ignition with a central spark plug. The exhausts were set in the V of the engine, as on a few examples of the 36-valve predecessor, and the inlets were now of the side-draught type, outside the heads and curved to minimise overall width. Ferrari claimed a power output of 403bhp for this engine and set Amon to make the best use of it in the race.

There was an outcry from the Italian press at Ferrari's mean-looking entry. It seemed to them a disgrace that only one Ferrari was entered for the Italian GP. They were outraged by the fact that it was driven by a foreigner. Ferrari's answer was that there were no professional Italian drivers left. Scarfiotti and Baghetti were part-timers and Bandini had been killed in a fiery and disastrously publicised crash at Monaco early in the year. As Ferrari pointed out, whenever an Italian driver was killed in a Ferrari the occasion was treated as a national disaster and Ferrari was treated as some kind of monster; whereas the Italian press seemed to have less compunction about letting foreign drivers kill themselves.

Amon drove superbly for the rest of the season. His new car was convincingly competitive at Watkins Glen and at Mexico City but on each occasion let him down with oil or fuel problems late in the race when he was doing really well.

Ferrari finished fourth in the constructors' championship again in 1968. This was a very interesting year and might have been interpreted as a stimulating one for Ferrari, for the cars went consistently well although they never won either the victories or the acclaim they deserved. Time and again Amon was fastest in practice, demonstrating conclusively that the car was at least as fast as anything that the opposition had to offer. With increasing frequency, as the new season wore on, Amon was abetted by his new young team-mate Ickx until by halfway through it was likely that one or the other would be in pole position on the starting grid. Ickx was either better or more fortunate in the actual races, with the result that he finished fourth in the world drivers' championship in front of Amon. What particularly helped him to this result was a tremendous win by a large margin in the French GP, an event which was run in the heavy rain which seems to suit Ickx as much as it disturbs Amon.

Throughout the year, the car remained the same 48-valve V12, except for practice before the Belgian GP when it was seen to be wearing a small airfoil above the engine. The Brabham was similarly equipped, and these two makes must take the credit for introducing a brilliantly simple device which was to have a shattering effect on racing car performance on a road or pseudo-road circuit. The idea was quite simple, and is now generally appreciated. By increasing the reaction between tyres and road the products of that reaction and the coefficient of friction between them can be increased and thus the potential cornering force magnified. Before the season was over, everybody had jumped on the bandwagon, and a profusion of airfoils, wings, flaps and other aerodynamic appendages appeared.

Perhaps the really significant thing about this introduction of the wing was that here, at long last, was Ferrari producing an innovation rather than merely copying what everybody else had established as desirable. It was symptomatic of a new spirit which seemed to enliven the technicians of Ferrari and which seemed correspondingly to encourage everybody else connected with the team. It was a trend which had begun in a small way with the passing of Dragoni from the position of team manager. He was succeeded by an amiable and considerate journalist, Franco Lini, who did much to improve the spirit in which the team's affairs were conducted. But it was perhaps most of all Forghieri and Rocchi to whom the credit should go for the new wave of technical advancement.

The quality of Rocchi's work could be seen in the new generation of V12 engines which propelled the Formula 1 cars and also the latest sports-racers. Apart from being big in bore and short in stroke – the product of simple impersonal logic – the engine had pressed-in cylinder liners which were wet in their upper halves and dry (that is, in direct contact with the block) over the lower half. These engines had little or nothing in common with their predecessors. Whereas the Colombo and Lampredi V12 crankcases finished in line with the crankshaft axis, Rocchi carried the skirts of his crankcase well below, adding immensely to the stiffness of the block, not only in beam, where the earlier engines were more than adequate already, but also in the planes at right angles thereto, where the others were not so good. Stiffness was further augmented by crossbolting of the main bearing caps which added more lateral bracing. This good practice seems habitual with Rocchi, being seen in his first production design, the special V6 prepared by Ferrari for the Fiat Dino.

There is Dino ancestry to be seen in the cylinder heads of these Rocchi V12s, too. In this case the Dino is the unraced Formula 2 engine referred to

Bandini in the 1½ litre flat 12

a little earlier, a 1½-litre machine of exceptionally low stroke: bore ratio (86 × 46 millimetres) which had its twin overhead camshafts very close to each other above each cylinder head; so close that they both lay beneath a common cover. They were close because they operated near-vertical valves, a choice of layout which Rocchi evidently made as early as Duckworth did in designing the Cosworth Ford V8. Like Duckworth, Rocchi arranged his combustion chambers so as to be partly accommodated within the piston crown and partly in the head. This was a three-valve arrangement, which made room for two sparking plugs per cylinder, each flanking the exhaust valve.

Remembering that 'he never made a mistake who never made anything,' we must go on to wonder whether Rocchi was perhaps too venturesome in developing the 1969 Grand Prix engine. This was a disastrous year, perhaps as bad as any that Ferrari had experienced in Formula 1 racing. It began optimistically enough, for Amon had a very successful winter winning the Tasman series of races. But disillusionment set in with the opening of the European Grand Prix season; and before the year was half completed, Amon was out of Grand Prix racing. Ickx had contracted himself to Brabham, and Ferrari's entries in the championship series were usually limited to one car, driven in the

92

of interest it was a particularly light engine, weighing only 344 lb – compared with 360 for the BRM V12 (which was admittedly more powerful) and 380 for the Cosworth V8 which was overwhelmingly successful. Further evidence of Ferrari's skill with the pruning pencil was the gearbox for this car, which weighed only 93 lb compared with 115 for the BRM and 122 for the Hewland gearbox which equipped all the other cars. The weight thus saved was to some extent squandered by a rugged chassis or hull structure; but the difference was such that the Ferrari was still one of the lightest cars to compete that year. The Lotus 49B, the BRM P138, and the Ferrari weighed between 1160 and 1163 lbs. Yet despite this lightness and power, the Ferrari seemed to lack the acceleration and responsiveness of its commoner rivals.

In other small details the 1969 GP car was quite attractive. The oil cooler, treated by other manufacturers as an afterthought which had to be hung somewhere in the wind, was surrounded in the Ferrari by an aerodynamic duct of properly divergent-convergent section, which reduced the drag induced by the cooler very considerably and improved its performance as a heat exchanger. Flanking it above the engine were the little airfoils still permitted in the regulations. The big and undoubtedly dangerous wings were banned with effect from the Monaco GP. The two halves of the permitted air foil on the Ferraris were independently adjustable for incidence and their ends bore plates which prevented or discouraged the vortex-inducing flow of air from the lower to the upper side of the air foil. These were pleasing little details, just as the hydraulically operated rams which adjusted the angle of incidence of the preceeding year's wing were; but such details do not win a race in the absence of the necessary stamina and power. So the year drew to an end with Ferrari fortunes and spirits sinking lower and lower. The only bright spot was a new 3-litre flat-12 engine which was intended to be intro-

latter half of the season by Rodriguez.

In the first race of the year, the Spanish GP, everything looked very promising. Amon was in the lead by half a minute and was all set to win when his engine seized. Thereafter he and his successor suffered repeated engine failures, which have been attributed to an over-zealous attempt to reduce friction by cutting down on bearing areas. At any rate the trouble was so rife that eventually the 1968 engine was substituted for the 1969 one, from which 435bhp was claimed. The essential external difference between the two engines was that the newer one had its porting reversed so that the inlets were within the sixty degrees of the V and the exhausts were on the flanks. As a matter

duced at Monza; but it blew itself up on the test bed, and everybody had to start again.

This engine was a continued source of trouble throughout the first half of 1970. The crankshaft was supported by four main bearings rather than the seven to which Ferrari had long been accustomed. It must not be overlooked that for an engine of such layout a four bearing crankshaft may be preferable.

was an expensive and time-consuming failure until the autumn of 1970 when all of a sudden it started winning races. Young Ickx, back with Ferrari for the year, turned out with this new car of fascinating construction and unchallengeable performance, and won four of the last five Grands Prix of the year.

One of the most refreshing things about this was relief from the monotony

The 65 degree V6 Ferrari formula 1 car pokes its Chiti nose around the Station hairpin at Monte Carlo

Where there is a main bearing between each crank throw, that bearing is subjected to the sum of the inertia loads on the adjacent throws; but in a four-bearing design the bearings are subjected only to the difference between those loads. Be that as it may, the flat 12

of having races won by kit cars powered by Cosworth. It also had an interesting engine, although the flat 12 configuration had been met on Ferrari before, as you will remember. But it was the chassis which attracted most attention – and how long is it since we have been able to say *that* about a Ferrari? Here the body was substantially a stressed skin monocoque structure, extending over the engine crankcase in the form of a cantilevered beam from which the engine hung. Such aerodynamic appendages as are permitted were employed; but an awareness of the importance of well-controlled air flow was shown by the careful ducting of divergent nozzles leading air to the twin oil coolers at the rear of the car.

There was, on the other hand, no evidence of free thinking on the subject of aerodynamics: one would never expect to see a Ferrari pioneering the cuneiform body shape with the same secessionist fervour as Lotus and Matra. Despite a most unapostolic succession of designers, each of whom changed something because it needed change and quite often changed for the sake of change, a Ferrari is always orthodox. It is always an example of the classical ideal in Grand Prix racing, whether one is considering the 1964 perpendicular model triumphing over the heterodoxy of Daimler-Benz at Silverstone, or the 1970 horizontal version gradually overcoming its particoloured rivals in the championship series of that year. Ferrari has never been tempted to abjure his national racing colours, nor to turn his cars into mobile advertisement hordings, for his cars have been above all things the embodiment of the old man's spirit, traditionalism, courage and taste. They have all been classical thoroughbreds, not ad-man's money-grubbers. With what pleasure did we see these classics gradually overcome the moderns: not until the fourth race of the 1970 champion series, the Belgian GP, did one finish impressively when the late Ignazio Giunti came fourth. In the next race, for the Dutch GP, Ickx was third and the other newcomer Clay Regaz-

zoni was fourth, with Ickx putting up the fastest lap. The next two races, the French and British, were again dominated by Lotus and Brabham, though Regazzoni brought the Ferrari 312B into fourth place at Brands Hatch. Then at Hockenheim for the German GP Ickx set the fastest lap and finished second behind Rindt's Lotus. The cars were finding both speed and reliability and within a fortnight they really had the bit between their teeth. Ickx and Regazzoni were first and second in the Austrian GP, and shared the fastest lap. Regazzoni won both honours in the Italian GP, and went on to achieve a record lap and come second in the Canadian race behind his team mate Ickx. In the next race, at Watkins Glen, it was the turn of Ickx to achieve a record lap, though in fourth place he was the highest Ferrari finisher. He was back in front at Mexico City with another fastest lap to his credit, Regazzoni finishing behind him in second place. And so the season ended. Rindt, killed in practice at Monza, had done well enough in the early part of the season to be world champion, but with forty points to his forty-five Ickx finished second in the listings and Regazzoni was third with thirty-three. This was despite the fact that the cars were really only competitive in the second half of the season.

In any case, a Ferrari is a Ferrari, not merely whatever vehicle so-and-so happens to be driving. In the constructors' championship Lotus, the Gaspers Special with engine by courtesy of Ford and transmission by Hewland, was the winner with 59 points. But the make that came second with 52 points was purely Ferrari. The credit for most of the design has been acribed to Forghieri, and its elegant simplicity certainly does him credit. It was not without its problems, as we have seen, the tendency of the early crankshafts to break being the main one. Certainly it was a highly stressed engine: its

John Surtees in the 1½ litre V8 formula 1 car

twelve cylinders, each of 78.5 millimetre bore and 51.5 millimetre stroke (comprehending 2991cc), defied the limitation of such geometry to run at a compression ration of 11.8:1 and realise 450bhp at 12,000 rpm. Not so long ago it was an exceptional 1½-litre engine that would rev as high as this, but with its two camshafts per head and four valves per cylinder the Ferrari 312B ran at a mean piston velocity of 4050 feet per minute when delivering its maximum power. At the time of writing we have seen nothing that can beat it.

THE RACING SPORTS CARS

The long and intricate history of Ferrari in Grand Prix racing is to a surprising degree the history of Ferrari in sports car racing as well. Ferrari's principle concern, as we have seen, has always been with engines: chassis have never been anything very special and the factory has always treated them with a certain amount of disdain, screwing engines in and out of them like light bulbs. When something went wrong with a Ferrari sports-racing car it was usually some part of the chassis or running gear, notably in the transmission department where rear axles, gearboxes and clutches were for years the Achilles heel of the competition cars – and indeed of the production cars as well.

The engines, though, were remarkably rugged: they could be broken by really brutal driving but it very seldom happened, because the engine was usually faster than the chassis, and the life that the driver sought to preserve was not that of the engine but his own. If he could keep it on the road, and with some of the more ferocious examples such as the 4.9-litre cars of the early 1950s this was no easy matter, the engine would still be howling its full fury at the end of a Mille Miglia or a 24-hour Le Mans race, just as surely as it would see its way through a 500 kilometre Grand Prix. It is a tribute to Colombo who started it all and to his successors that what had been right for the ephemeral frenzy of a Grand Prix, even up to 1957 when such machinery ran on extravagant brews of alcoholic composition, was also right for the long-distance sports-car racing classics.

So when Ferrari's rivals sometimes complained that his sports cars were simply Grand Prix machines with lights and an extra seat, they were often right in principle though they were not necessarily right in particulars. On occasions, indeed, a Ferrari sports car *was* simply a Grand Prix car without

This early Spyder with Type 212 engine was driven by Stagnoli in the 1953 Targa Florio

even an extra seat, but merely with a different body. The most fetching example must be the 4½-litre V12 Grand Prix car that was retrieved from the 1951 GP establishment and rebodied as a monoposto sports car for Rosier and Trintignant. In most cases the similarity between the sports racers and GP types was less unequivocal; but apart from mild detuning, such as lowering the compression ratio and running on petrol instead of alcohol, there was little difference in the engines. Quite often they were increased in capacity to take advantage of the different limits applying in sports car racing, so that we often find the two-seaters faster than the single seaters – an achievement in which they were aided of course by bodywork which was usually more aerodynamic and seldom sufficiently heavier as to be a real handicap.

Ferrari's first post-war cars, as we have seen, were the Colombo-designed type 125, a 1½-litre V12 which came in three assorted degrees of tune. When the FIA introduced Formula 2 racing for single seaters with unsupercharged 2-litre engines, the Ferrari V12 was expanded to make the type 166 2-litre model, and in a simple chassis with a live rear axle this made the first classic competition Ferrari sports car. In 1948 it won the Mille Miglia, driven by Biondetti; and in the following year he not only repeated this success but won the combined Tour of Sicily and Targa Florio as well.

The car was one of the prettiest front-engined two-seaters ever, dressed in a Superleggera body by Touring. It was a compact, all-enveloping, slab-sided, gently-contoured design nicknamed the 'Barchetta' and it set a lasting fashion, being copied unashamedly by Tojeiro, Cooper and AC. It was one of these which made Ferrari internationally famous by winning the Le Mans race in 1949, and siring younger and lustier progeny such as the bored-out type 195 Sport of 1950.

This was just the start of a rush towards the goal of superabundant power. For in that same year Ferrari dispensed with the little Colombo V12 for GP racing and the big unblown Lampredi V12 took over to give the Alfa Romeos a run for their money and eventually, in 1951, to beat them. The 4½-litre GP began as a 3.3-litre prototype; and in this size it made its sports car debut in the same event as the Colombo-based type 195. It was tremendously fast in this Mille Miglia, but was put out by rear axle failure.

From then until 1956, Ferrari's interests were represented in sports car competition by a mixed bag of cars whose engines showed an amazing variety of size and detail although they were always unmistakable Ferrari V12s. Those based on the Colombo design grew from 1½-litres to 2.3, 2.6, 2.7, 2.9, 3.3 or 4-litres; the Lampredi engines, with their longer blocks and cylinder liners screwed into the heads, ran from 3-litres through 3.3, 4.1, and 4.5 to 4.9-litres, the last producing 344bhp at 6,500 rpm. This was enough to give a Spider-bodied two-seater commanding acceleration, enough to make its control in difficult circumstances embarrassingly tricky, but enough to let it win some important events, most notably the 1954 Le Mans race.

Meantime Ferrari had found other work for Lampredi's hands to do, in designing the new four-cylinder engines for the Grandes Epreuves of 1954 and 1955, (which were run according to Formula 2 regulations) and those of succeeding years to which the new 2½-litre Formula 1 applied. So successful were these engines that their application to sports-racing cars was as inevitable as had been the case with the preceeding V12s: the original 2-litre car became in two-seater form the type

The Barchetta body by Superleggera Touring was universally and deservedly popular. This example had a 2.3 litre Type 195 engine for the 1952 Targa Florio. Driver Mathieson is talking to Cav. Vincenzo Florio

A Type 212 Barchetta at Le Mans in 1951 just after leaving the road and overturning

500 Mondial, giving 170bhp at 7,000 rpm on a compression ratio of 9.2:1. After an initial experiment which consisted simply in dropping a 2½-litre Grand Prix engine into a type 166 Mille Miglia car, the type 625 engine was increased in size to a full 3-litres, when it became the type 750 Monza. The type 860 Monza was enlarged to 3.4-litres, giving 280bhp at 6,000 rpm compared with 260 at 6,400 from the type 750.

For a time these cars were immensely successful, exhibiting the abundance of torque at relatively low speeds which had made the Lampredi fours so effective in Grand Prix racing, especially on the slower circuits. In 1954 and 1955 the experiment was prolonged, and the in-line fours were supplemented by in-line sixes. Thus the 3.7-litre type 118LM was a Mondial with two extra cylinders of the same size as the type 625 Formula 1 engine. This was

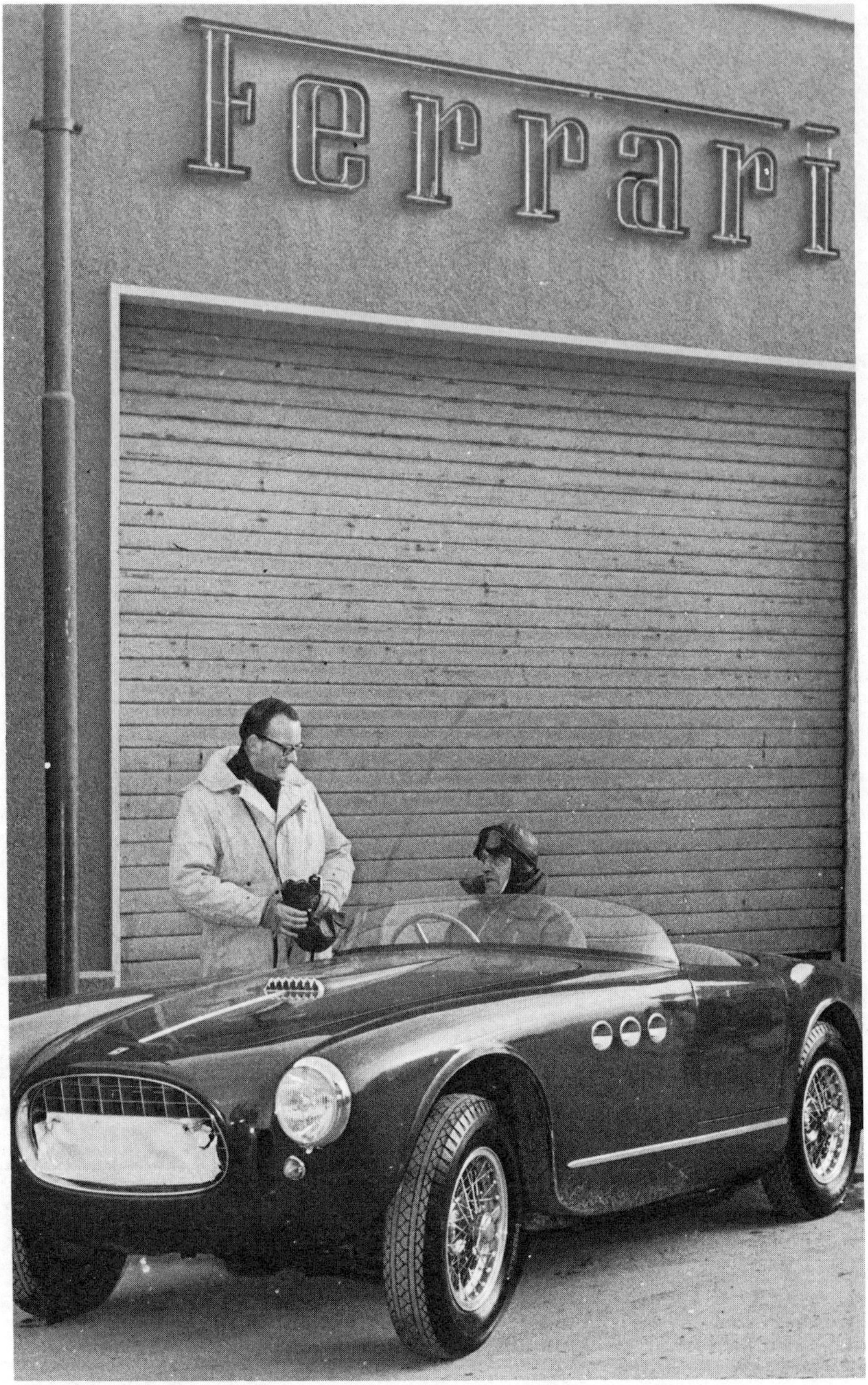
Ferrari

to power a very fast car, its 280bhp making it competitive with the 4.9-litre V12 in the 1000 kilometres race at Buenos Aires and allowing Taruffi to win the Tour of Sicily. Then for the Mille Miglia came an in-line six that was an absolute paralyser: the type 121LM, with bore and stroke of 102 and 90 millimetres respectively, amounting to 4.4-litres and capable of 360bhp.

It had to be good. In 1955 the full technocratic might of Daimler-Benz was applied to the domination of the classic long-distance sports car races, just as it had already begun to be dominant in Grand Prix racing. For the 1955 Mille Miglia the complex and superbly engineered straight-eight Mercedes-Benz was considered a threat not merely to Ferrari but to the very hon-

One of the most rudimentary of Michelotti's designs for Vignale bodies was this 1952 specimen executed on the 4.1 litre Type 340 Mexico chassis

When Vignale produced a really superb body in the first 2.9 litre V12, the Type 250 Mille Miglia, its shape was adapted by Pininfarina to produce this staple of the mid-fifties, distinguishable from the Vignale body by its windscreen: the earlier car had rounded top corners to the glass

our of Italy. Ferrari's answer lay in type 118LMs for four drivers and a single 121LM for the dashing young Castellotti. At Ravenna Castellotti was ahead, having averaged 119mph, two minutes quicker than Moss in the Mercedes-Benz; but he was forced to retire, as did two of the other Ferraris, and Maglioli who brought his type 118 into third place received scant attention amidst all the acclaim for Mercedes-Benz and Moss, who had achieved what every Italian had been brought up to believe impossible.

Things went no better for the remainder of the year. Le Mans was a

103

disaster and, even without the tragic accident which marred it, would still have been a fiasco as far as Ferrari was concerned: Castellotti's 121 led for the first hour before going out with overheating, to be followed by the remainder of the team. In Sweden for the sports car GP, in Britain for the Tourist Trophy, in Sicily for the Targa Florio, Mercedes-Benz prevailed every time, though in this last event Castellotti lost second place only through having to stop to change a flat tyre. In so doing he was forced to lose the precious point that cost Ferrari the sports car championship for 1955.

It had been altogether a terrible year, in sports car racing and in Grands Prix. Ferrari himself had lost confidence in the ability and dependability of any engine mustering fewer than twelve cylinders, and even went

In a Viganale-bodied Type 340MM, Giannino Marzotto starts his winning drive in the 1953 Mille Miglia

In this 250MM Gerini finished third in the 1954 Tour of Sicily

so far as to reintroduce a 4.9 V12 for one or two races towards the end of the year. But then came the surprise offer of the Lancia racing cars and engineers, and he began to think again. The engineers included Jano and Massimino, who seem to have been made welcome, while it was made clear to Lampredi that Ferrari had no further use for his services.

What must he have thought therefore when he observed the introduction of a new four-cylinder 2-litre Ferrari christened the Testa Rossa (simply because its cam covers were crackle-painted red) in April 1956? The car was largely a development of Lampredi's 2-litre Mondial, stimulated by a new 2-litre capacity limit for many of the more popular sports car races (such as the 1000 kilometres event at Monza) due to widespread fears that sports cars were getting too fast and powerful – fears

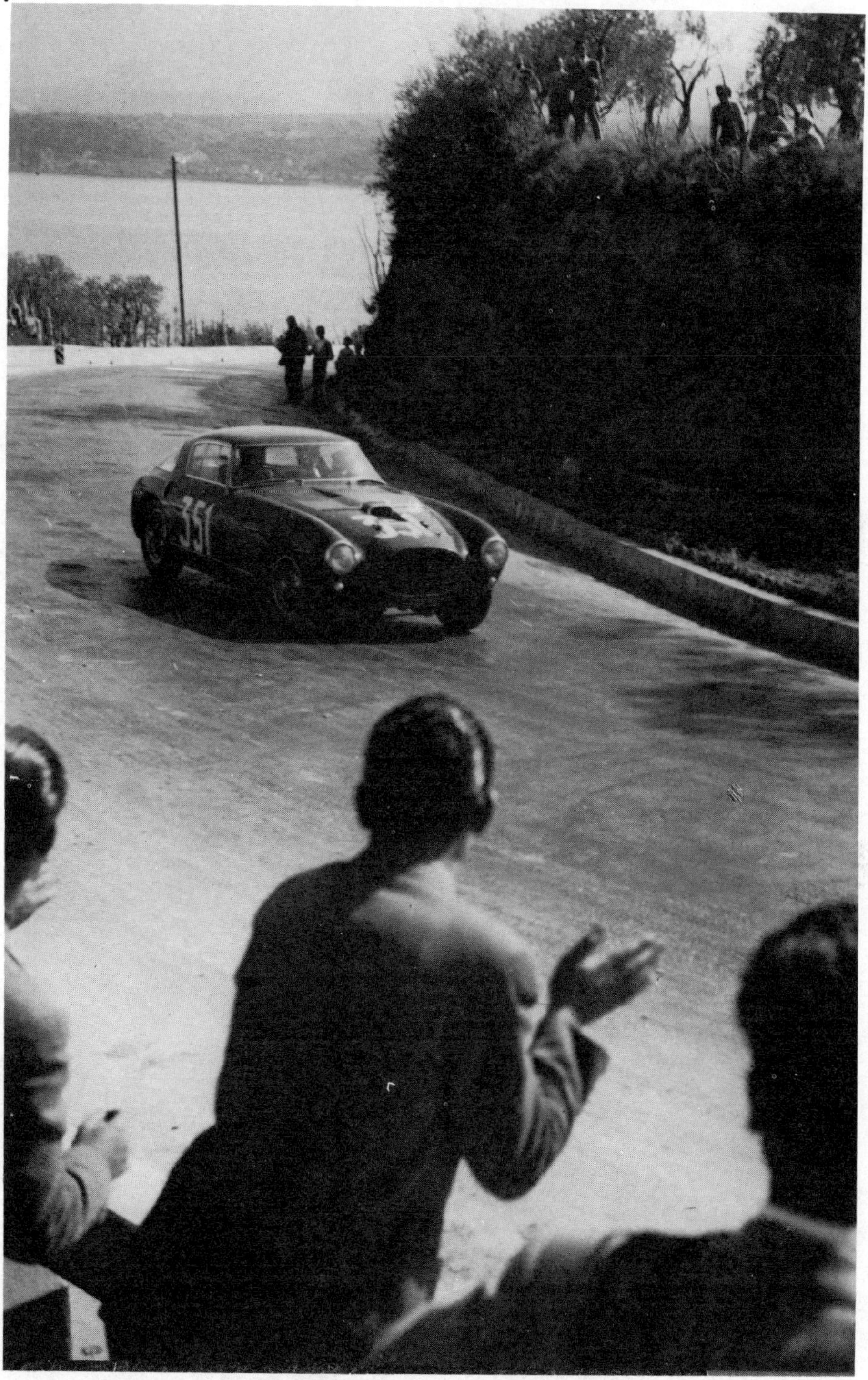
351

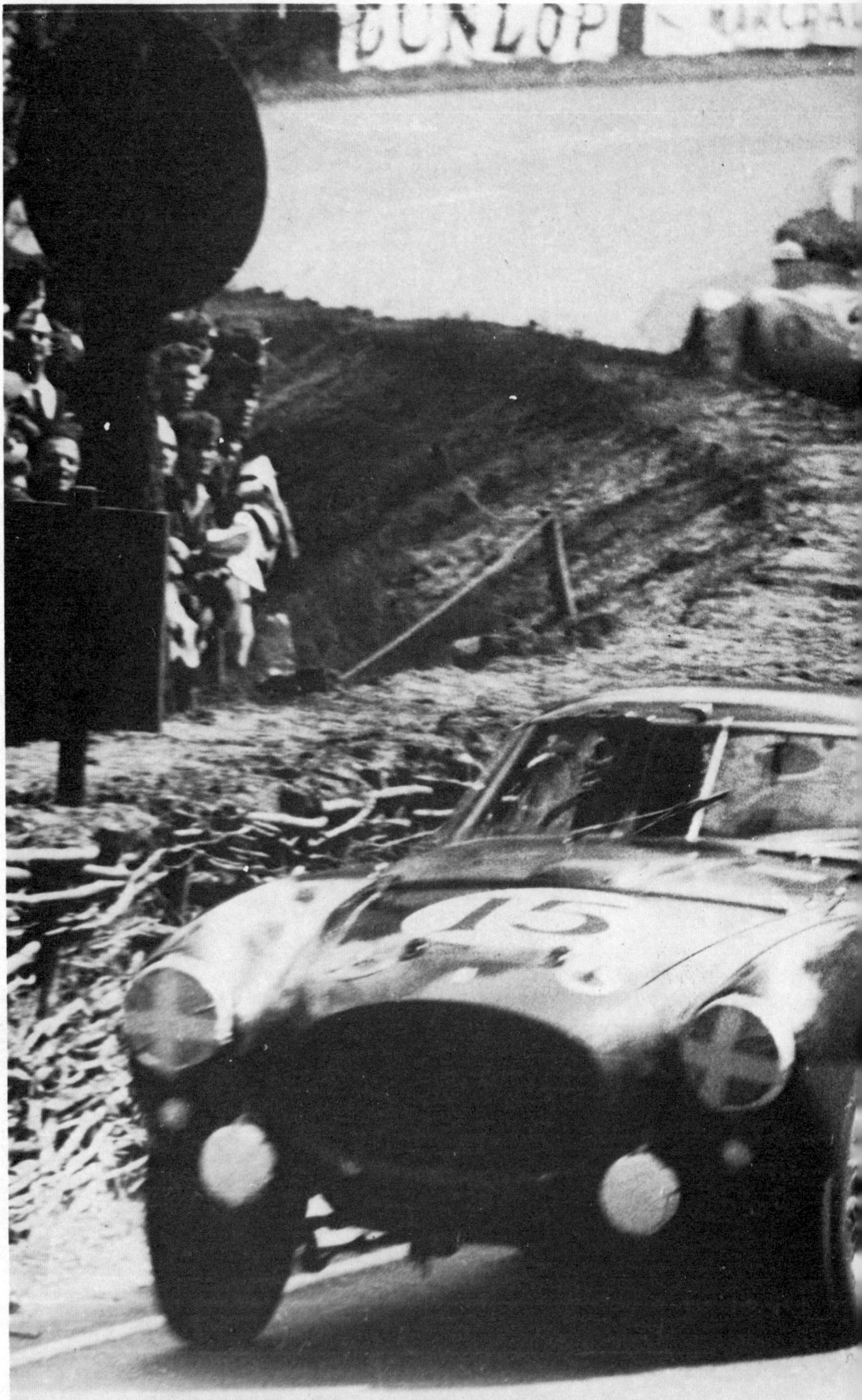
DUNLOP

Le Mans 1953, and one of the factory-entered Ferrari coupes leads Aston Martin DB3S, Cunningham and Jaguar C-type through Les Esses. Looking like 250MM cars, the Ferraris had 4.1 or 4.5 litre engines

Le Mans 1954, and Ferrari wins: Gonzales, Trintignant and their Types 375 Plus spyder, festooned with jubilant mechanics

that had been expressed with more emotion than logic ever since the accident at Le Mans the previous year. The development work and general redesign had been done by Ferrari's new engineering team which consisted not only of Jano and Massimino but also of Bellantani and the young Andrea Fraschetti, whose promising career was cut short when he was killed at Modena track while test driving the 1958 Dino. This team had not only revised the engine but also the chassis: in its meteoric career the Mondial/Monza series had grown up from an old-fashioned chassis with transverse leaf springing at the front and a live axle at the rear, until eventually it had coil springs at the front and a de Dion rear suspension with the gearbox incorporated with the final drive. Now the Testa Rossa reverted to an engine-mounted gearbox and a live rear axle, albeit one that was located by parallel trailing arms and sprung by coils. But again, like the early Mondial, the Testa Rossa was initially a success.

The Mondial had been an overnight sensation when it finished second overall in the Mille Miglia at its first appearance; the Testa Rossa was first, third and fourth in the Monza race of 1956, and made as much impact. A month later it appeared with a 2½-litre engine that was virtually the type 625GP unit. Little was achieved with this car by the factory, and not a great deal was attempted; but the Testa Rossa was a very successful car as far as the customers were concerned, and was made in fair numbers, either as two or 2½-litre, 1956 and 1957.

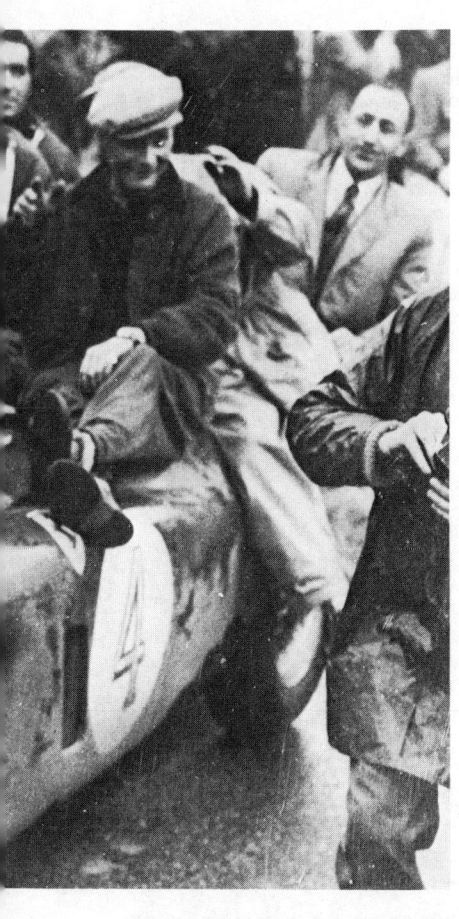

In the meantime the Ferrari engineers had been busying themselves with a new V12 engine. While still on their way towards becoming production car manufacturers in the accepted sense, they had been dithering between the Colombo V12 and the Lampredi V12, but finally they made up their minds to combine the best features of both in a new engine which powered their 1956 Mille Miglia type 290. This engine was a purely racing one, with 24 spark plugs, dry sump lubrication, hairpin valve springs, greatly enlarged valves and 320bhp from 3.5-litres. In spider two-seater bodies designed by Pininfarina and built by Scaglietti (whom young Dino Ferrari had introduced to Ferrari custom) they were the epitome of the handsome well-bred front-engined hyper-sports car; and their domination of the Mille Miglia, which was run in a torrential rain storm, was as complete aesthetically as it was morally and physically. Further developed, the four-camshaft V12s were equally successful in the following year – and yet their ascendancy was brief. The Colombo V12 was making a comeback.

Back among the production cars, the Lampredi engine had been finally superseded and the older V12 revived in 3-litre form to produce the type 250 GT. More or less simultaneously the motor sporting world became very chary of out-and-out rabid racing two-seaters, and pandered to the popular distaste for such 'monsters' by developing a new class of racing for grand touring cars. For this the 250GT Ferrari was to the manner born, and over the next couple of years it was shown that the roadgoing 3-litre engine of the 250 GT was quite capable of standing up to the demands of long-distance racing. In 1957 a 250GT Berlinetta finished third in the Mille Miglia, driven by Gendebien and powered by an engine that was basically standard, albeit well tuned. This made the potential of the revised Colombo design obvious; and when it was given the generous twelve-throated carburation that it lacked in its early days, it was clearly an engine that was capable of great power as well as maintaining exemplary reliability.

Both these attributes were eagerly sought after by Ferrari, who was suffering as never before from the stiffness of competition from Jaguar, Aston Martin and others. What finally made up his mind was the determination by the FIA to impose a 3-litre capacity limit on sports cars taking part in the major events of 1958.

Thus was born the type 250 Testa Rossa, virtually a highly developed version of the 250 GT V12 with improved porting, outside plugs, six twin-throat carburettors, fiercer camshafts, and dry-sump lubrication. Ferrari claimed that the useful rpm range extended from as low as 1500 to 7800, taking in a power peak of 300bhp on the way at 7200 rpm. But, and this was an occasion so rare and so important as to deserve emphasis, it was not a Grand Prix engine. In 1958 Ferrari's GP cars were dependent on the new Dino V6 engine; and instead of fielding sports cars similarly powered, he was relying on an uprated production engine.

It was a pretty and effective car into which this engine went. The prototype

For a few brief years the four-and six-cylinder sports-racing Ferraris were successful and prodigiously fast. Biggest of the fours was the 3½-litre Type 960 Monza (easily distinguished by the cambox clearance blisters) here nearing victory in the hands of Fangio at Sebring in 1956

The V12 Type 290MM was faster than the 860 Monza, but this superiority was not always reflected by race results. At the Nurburgring in 1956 this one, driven by the Marquis de Portago, Ken Wharton, Phil Hill and Olivier Gendebien, finished third behind the second-place Monza 860 of Fangio and Castellotti – who were the factory's fastest drivers

250TR of 1957, with its shapely and surprising Scaglietti body, had a multitube chassis frame derived from the earlier four-cylinder Testa Rossa, the wheelbase measuring 92½ inches. Front suspension was coil-sprung independent, the rear incorporated a live axle and leaf springs, and the whole thing weighed 730 kg. By the 1958 season the live rear axle had given way to a de Dion system with coil springs, and a revised body – smoother and with a lower drag coefficient – appeared in May of that year in time for the Targa Florio. As the year went on the experi-

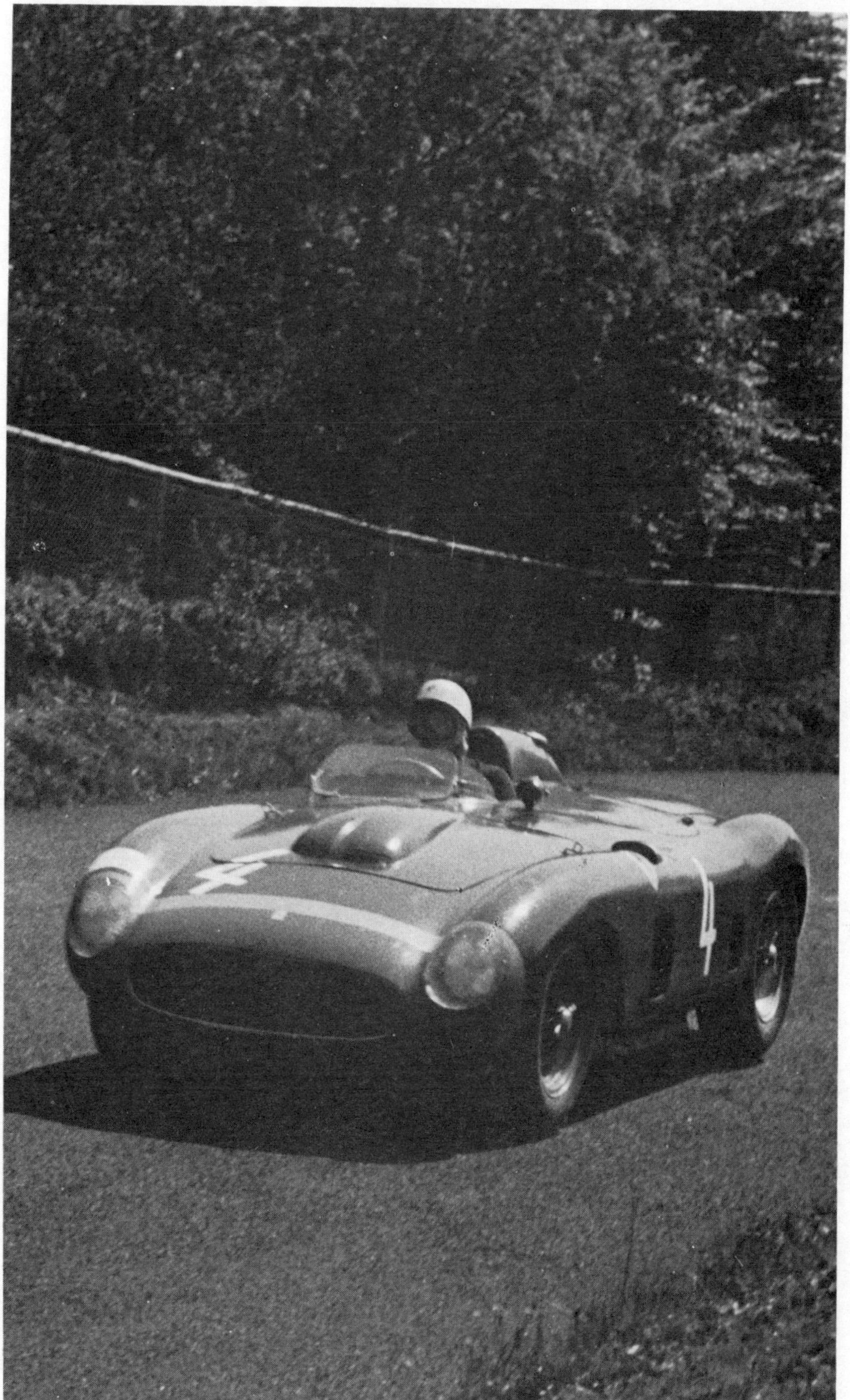

ments continued with gearboxes hanging on the back of the engine or combined with the final drive, with old bodies and new ones, with various types of carburettor air intakes on top of the shallow bonnet, with left-hand drive and right-hand . . . and with a general level of success which brought Ferrari the world sports car championship for the third time in succession and the fifth since its inception in 1953.

Briefly the 250TR was a tremendous success, earning in 1958 nearly twice as many points as either Aston Martin or Porsche who finished equal second in the championship. For 1959 the car was to develop even further, being given disc brakes at long overdue last, a new lightweight tubular frame with the engine offset therein, and with a number of minor variations in transmission and bodywork. It was not quite such a good year, Ferrari just being pipped for the championship by Aston Martin who had the benefit of Moss driving for them, and managing nothing better than third place at Le Mans – a third place that significantly enough was taken by a 250GT, which lasted when the prototypes did not. For the following year the Testa Rossa had a dry sump engine, just for safety's sake. Some examples also had independent rear suspension, and bodily the cars were distinguished by the dreadful high windscreen upon which regulations insisted for that year. Still the car went campaigning successfully, its bodywork being amended in the following year so as to make the best out of the bad job which its higher windscreen undoubtedly was.

This was a period in which motor sport and motor engineering were undergoing tremendous and far-reaching changes, a period in which the Grand Prix car suffered a complete metamorphosis and in which the sports car began uncertainly to follow the same trend. The rear-engined sports-racing car was bound to come, and the obvious way to make a start on it would be with a two-seater version of the rear-engined Dino that first made its appearance among the single-seaters late in 1960. To ensure that the engine would be up to it, a Dino-engined version of the TR was tried as early as 1958, and was campaigned with increasing enthusiasm in subsequent years. Still the front-engined V12 persevered through 1960, and to a large extent in 1961. Even in 1962 it was a development of it which was run at Le Mans, for in that year there was a category for 4-litre prototypes which Ferrari found irresistible: by bringing the 400 Super America production engine up to Testa Rossa standard and putting it in a spider-bodied two-seater of peculiar ugliness, he achieved what he set out to do. Yet he might have saved himself the trouble, for second to this short-lived prototype was a Grand Touring Ferrari, the superb new 250GTO, still with the classic Colombo single-camshaft (per bank) V12 engine in front, still the most compellingly beautiful and elegant of all fast cars, the one to set standards by which all the others might be judged.

The 250GTO went on getting better and even more beautiful right through to the end of 1964, but in the meantime Ferrari tried a typical piece of regression: having put another of his hot 4-litre engines in a GTO for Le Mans and the Nurburgring in 1962 he then installed a similar engine in what was called the 330LMB, in effect a Berlinetta Lusso with a GTO nose and raised sheet metal covers over the rear wheel arches to give more clearance for oversized tyres – a detail last seen on the team cars a decade earlier. The steel-bodied LMB at Le Mans in 1963 weighed 1270kg, the heaviest car there; maybe that is why it had clutch troubles and could only finish fifth, though it had broken the existing lap record in practice. Ahead of it were four other Ferraris, a splendid smack in the eye for those who argued that what Ferrari needed was to be bought out by Ford, as Ford had tried to do a little earlier. Of these four Ferraris, two were GTOs in second and fourth places, and the other two the new rear-engined 3-litre V12 prototype, the 250P.

Of course the rear-engined Ferrari sports car had to come. The main question was how long it would take, for the old man was still reluctant to follow the herd, though not as stubbornly resistant to change as he had once been.

In fact the change to rear engines was a fairly long drawn out process which began in 1961 with the introduction of the Dino 246 sports prototype. This was a design based on the rear-engined V6 Grand Prix car, and was bodied in an impressive new style with a high rear deck wrapped over the roll-over protection cage, with the windscreen swept around the sides of the cockpit to mate with the deck and give the effect of a roofless coupe. The car was first raced at Sebring, where it led until a steering arm broke. Clearly this was an extremely fast car, and its promise was confirmed by winning the Targa Florio and by contending for the lead at Le Mans until it ran out of fuel on the circuit due to a miscalculation of its consumption. If its career was chequered, its performance was never in doubt: while it was current the 246SP Dino was one of the very fastest sports cars in competition.

Indeed all the little Dini were incredibly fast – though some of them were only superficially little: the series included a 2862cc V6 (the 286SP) and a rare V8 of 2½-litres known as the 248SP, designed by Chiti with a view to easing the spares and service problems, for many of its components were common to the 400 Super America engine. Only two of these are believed to have been built and they did not do a great deal, whereas the V6 cars were abundant and busy throughout the 1960s. In particular the 2-litre versions were amazingly fast, the most prodigious performance being perhaps the way they gave chase to the Chaparral during the Nurburgring 1000 kilometres race in 1966.

On all occasions these exquisite little cars clearly handled superbly, and when they were going well they were extremely fast, but they never enjoyed the development and preparation that they deserved and their reliability was always questionable. Whether they would have fared better in the continued presence of Chiti is debatable, but after a monumental row that accomplished boffin had quit Maranello in 1961, taking several other engineers with him – which is why his trademark, the twin-nostril nose, disappeared from the cars that he had designed in subsequent years. Where stamina was at a discount and speed and handling at a premium, the Dini did very well, notably in the European hillclimb championship, first snatched from Porsche by Scarfiotti in 1962.

Late in that year a Dino 246SP chassis was taken and stretched, and a V.12 engine was installed. It appeared at Monza for testing by John Surtees, and during this (his first drive in a Ferrari sports car) he broke the lap record. Here indeed was a promising new machine, new but trustworthy because the old type 250 Testa Rossa engine was there to protect the Ferrari reputation. All that remained to do was to get rid of the Chiti nose and in the process evolve a new Pininfarina body design, and there it was – a compact well proportioned two-seater weighing 690kg, developing 310bhp, and capable of sustaining high speeds for as long as was necessary. In its first race twelve hours were enough, Surtees and Scarfiotti driving the car to victory at Sebring in March 1963. Another finished second, a front-engined TR was third and 250GTO Berlinettas took fourth, fifth, sixth and other assorted places.

It certainly looked as though the Ferrari star was in the ascendant, and when Surtees lapped the Le Mans circuit during the spring trials at over 133 mph, representing a reduction on the existing record of nearly twelve seconds, that impression was confirmed. The 250P could hardly fail to draw considerable attention if it were capable of such performance, for Ferrari had emphasised that it was a genuine prototype, and when the car was first shown

Above: Scaglietti's prototype body for Dino Ferrari's own car led the way for a new style in sports-racing spyders. Below: Ferrari No 8, the Type 335S, leads away from the start at Le Mans in 1957. Highest placed Ferrari at the finish was fifth, but a 335S set a new 126mph lap record. Right: Four- and six-cylinder Ferraris, in sizes ranging from the 2-litre 500 Mondial to the 4.4-litre 121 LM and all looking very similar, were popular in America in the mid-fifties – but not when, as here at Sebring, they ran out of road

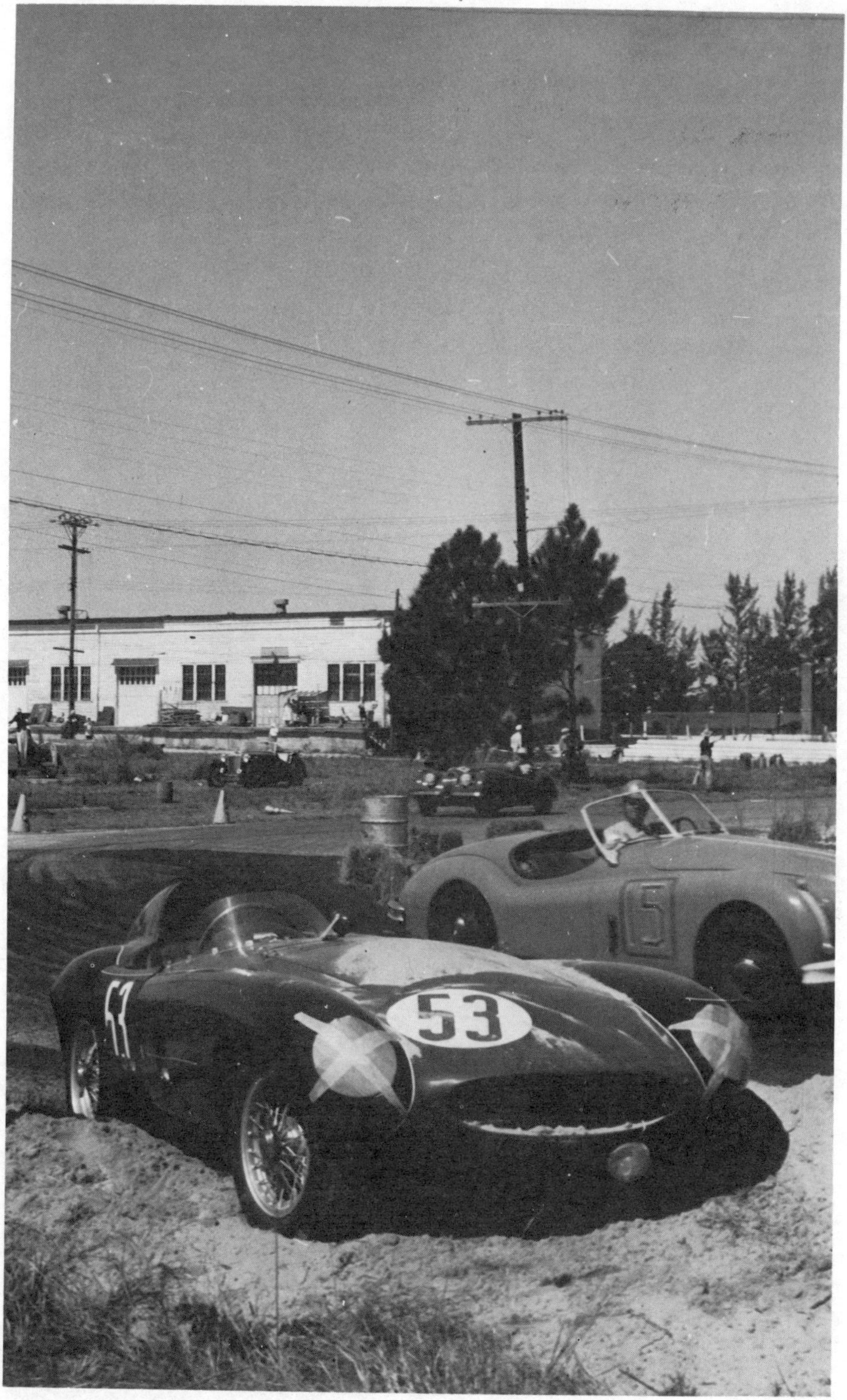
53
5

The Type 500 Testa Rossa engine of 1956. Location of the starter on the bell housing shows that the crankcase derives from the Lampredi GP engines

it was finished accordingly with complete trim (even to a glass windscreen) and an air of ruggedness which gave the lie to notions that this was a thinly disguised racer or sprint car, and showed it to be a serious design for production. On the whole the 250P had a good year in competition in 1962, winning at a variety of circuits besides Le Mans, and Ferrari was already taking orders for the production GT version which he was calling the 250 Berlinetta Le Mans or 250LM for short. It had been given a roof with buttress sail panels projecting aft of the vertical rear window, a roof essentially similar to that which graced its contemporary 250GTO equivalent. In this form and and with a clutch mounted to the engine flywheel rather than behind the transmission as in the racing version, the car was shown to the public at Brussels, London and Turin. Unfortunately Ferrari ran into terrible difficulties with the FIA who refused to homologate the car, remaining unconvinced that he had built as many as the rules required. The situation was not made any less complicated by the fact that all except the original 250LM example had a 3.3-litre engine, the cylinder bore having been increased from 73 to 77 millimetres so that the car should by rights have been called the 275LM, as it often is by many authorities. Nevertheless Ferrari insisted that it be called the 250LM in order not to confuse the homologation issue. even further. Whether he was right so to do is questionable, but the car was not homologated for 1964 as he had hoped.

Whatever the legal justification, this refusal must be seen now as a pity, for the car had immense promise, and had it been accepted as a production grand tourer it could have achieved even more than in fact it did. Not until 1966 was homologation grudgingly granted, and by then it was too late for the car to make its impact. Admittedly a number of racing versions were built and sold to private entrants who must have been agreeably surprised by its ability to give a good account of itself even when several years old. Indeed it was a privately entered 3.3-litre 250LM which saved Ferrari's reputation at Le Mans in 1965, when all the factory prototypes had expired after breaking the formidable opposition presented by the 7-litre Fords and it was left to an American-entered car driven by Gregory and Rindt to win, with similar cars taking 2nd and 6th places.

In the meantime Ferrari had to think again about his sports-racing prototypes, for although the 250P was an excellent proposition as the basis for a new generation of grand touring Berlinettas, it was not sufficiently extreme in its specification to have any hopes of remaining competitive in the major sports car races where the pace was increasing so rapidly. In short it was a strong car, as Ferrari's sports cars have nearly always been, but in view of current developments it might not be a fast enough car. Ford, having failed to buy Ferrari, were now committed to beating him, and set about the task with all possible elaboration and extravagance. The Ferrari answer to this threat for 1964 competition consisted of two new versions of the rear-engined V12 prototype, longer, sleeker and bigger engined. One was the 275P, carrying the established 3.3 V12 engine, the other was the 330P, its 4-litre engine giving 370bhp although the car was heavier and less handy than its less powerful companion. Between them they had a successful season, proving jointly unbeatable in the prototype class

Another view of the 2-litre four-cylinder Testa Rossa. The camboxes are not unlike those of the Type 625

Above: The 1958 Test Roassa prototype under construction. Below: Inside any Ferrari, even this Scaglietti 250 TR prototype, essentials such as the wheel, gearlever, handbrake and flasher switch are always recognizably the same

Above: Ferrari was obstinate about disc brakes. The original V12 Testa Rossa had these liberally stiffened drum-type brakes. Below: Finished, but soon to be modified: the original Type 250 TR

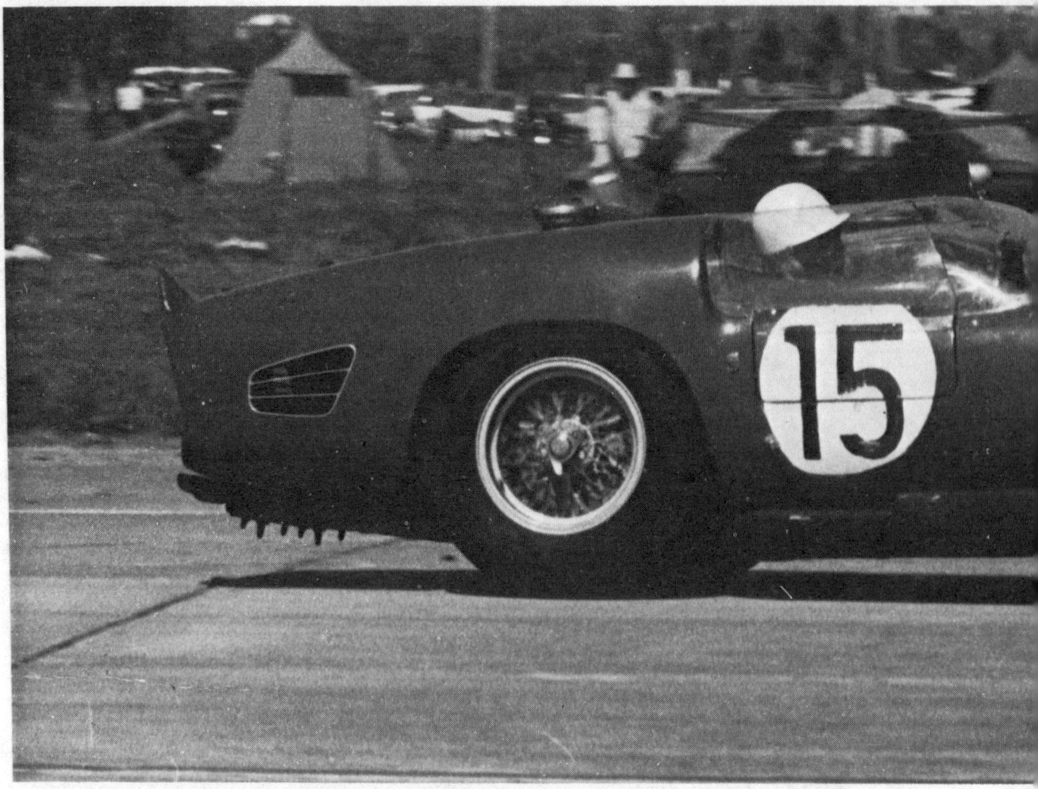
15

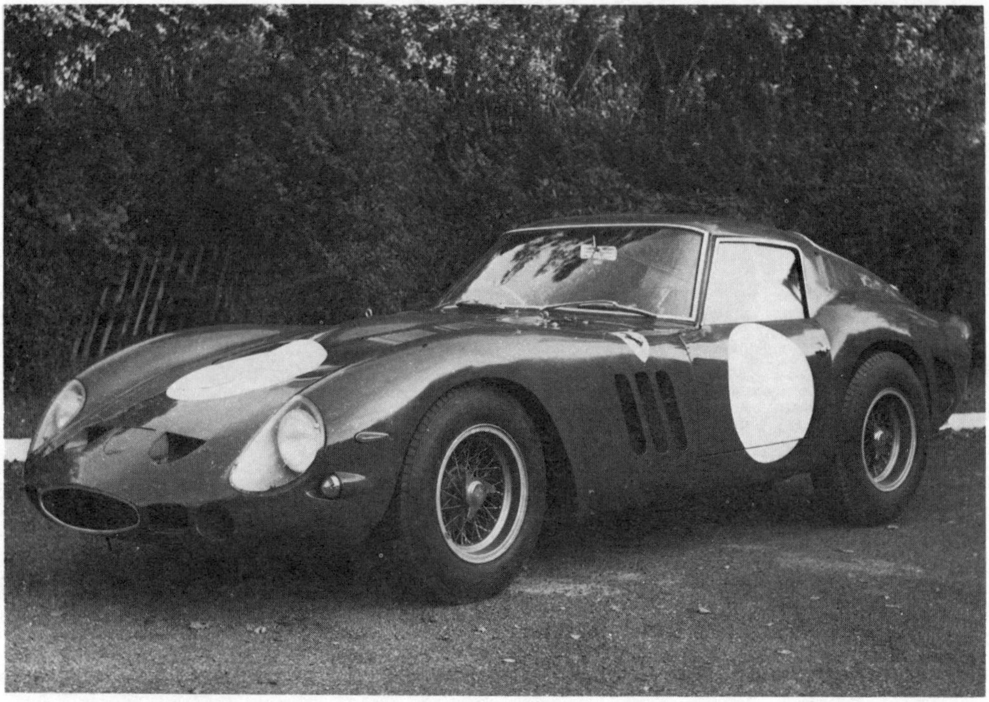

where the new Ford GT40 was a conspicuous failure.

For the following year more progress would be necessary, for the Ford was equally conspicuous for its speed for as long as it lasted. This was, then, the occasion for the first wholly new sports car since the days of Chiti. The chassis was new, being a semi-monocoque design after the fashion of the successful 1964 Grand Prix car: stressed sheet metal was rivetted to and supplemented the light multi-tubular framework. The suspension was exactly similar in its principles to what was now accepted as normal in Grand Prix cars, and even the engine was in a sense new. Strictly speaking, however, it was a development of the four-camshaft 1956 type 290 Mille Miglia whose dimensions had been altered in 1957 to give it a capacity of 4023cc. Finally,

Compellingly beautiful and elegant, yet brutally fast, the Ferrari GTO set the standard by which such cars are judged

First appearance of the transverse spoiler lip across the tail of a car in competition was on this 250 TR 60 at Sebring in 1961, when it finished second in the hands of Mairesse and Baghetti

the body was completely new. No longer was the design entrusted to Pininfarina; instead the factory developed the shape in its own wind tunnel. The result looked not unlike the little Dino.

This car, the 330P2, started off badly at Daytona and Sebring in 1965, failing abysmally on each occasion while the American cars did well. The P2 was hurriedly modified in time for the Le Mans trials, appearing with magnesium wheels in place of the old-fashioned wire-spoked type and with a new five-speed gearbox. With it Surtees raised the lap record to 139.9mph and was timed at 190 on the Mulsanne straight. Morale in the Ferrari camp was further increased by victory for the P2 at Nur-

121

A Scaglietti short-wheelbase Berlinetta 250GT of 1959/61 pattern, driven by Sterling Hamil in an American event

burgring; and then, as we have seen, it broke the Ford opposition at Le Mans so that by the third hour Ferraris occupied the first five places. At about breakfast time on the second day, however, gearbox troubles eliminated both the 330 P2s and, as recounted earlier, it was a 250LM that won. Meantime a number of P2 cars had been equipped with single camshaft 4.4-litre engines for customers, and these 365 P2s did as much to uphold the Ferrari reputation as the factory cars.

It was a fair year, but Ferrari knew that he was racing against time as well as against money (the Americans were pouring fortunes into their efforts to win at Le Mans) and while tradition maintained that this could not be done in less than three years, the third year was now imminent. So the 330 P2 was redesigned, making the most of relaxations in regulations about windscreens so as to produce a dramatically beautiful new body of greatly improved penetration, reduced frontal area and lower weight. The engine was still the 4-litre four-cam device used in 1965, but a higher compression ratio and the adoption of Lucas fuel injection brought the power up to date to 420bhp at 8000 rpm. The factory said it would do 193mph, and one look at the car made this seem a conservative estimate. Certainly it was very fast, and when the P3 made its racing debut at Sebring it led for a time but had to retire when the gear lever broke. This particular car was a spider, but the Berlinetta appeared at Monza for the 1000 kilometres race, which was also the occasion of the return to racing of John Surtees after recovering from the serious injuries he sustained in a crash in Canada in 1965. The elements combined to mark the occasion with a deep purple rainstorm that made floodlights necessary for the pit straight, caused windscreen wiper problems to plague most cars and Ferraris in particular, but did not stop the P3 from winning and setting fastest lap. In fact rain made a mess of many of the big sports-car races in 1966, falling very heavily during the first half of the Targa Florio in which Bandini overturned the P3 while in the lead.

At the Nurburgring, rain made the final laps very dramatic, with the Chaparral stopping to have fitted the first example of broad-grooved rain tyres to be seen in racing. While these fancy Firestones were being fitted the little 2-litre Dino was rapidly catching up, but alas for the P3, it suffered repeated damper troubles and finally retired with a burned-out clutch, although it had made fastest lap.

Surtees, who drove it, was having his last race for Ferrari, though he was not aware of this at the time. Amongst all the other troubles that beset the team as Le Mans approached (labour troubles at the factory prevented the cars from being properly prepared, and it has been said that the P3 had barely been touched) a flaming row brewed up between Surtees and racing manager Dragoni, the issue seeming trivial in retrospect but really being the last straw in a back-breaking process that had begun much earlier. Ferrari supported Dragoni and Surtees left. Even had he stayed, the result would probably have been the same: the ill-prepared Ferraris all retired, and with the expiration of the three years' apprenticeship and the expenditure of a staggering amount of money, Ford won. In a showmanlike finish Ford came second and third as well, and won the manufacturers' championship, leaving nothing much to fight for.

So Ferrari did very little in the remainder of the season, apart from engineer Rocchi designing a new V12 for the Grand Prix cars which did so well in the Monza GP. In December a new P4 prototype was sent to Daytona for a practice session, and this car had a 4-litre version of the new Rocchi engine. It gave no less than 450bhp at 8000 rpm; and when this power was combined with the new aerodynamic slipperiness of the body and the formidable properties of the new super-wide Firestone tyres, which required widened wheel arches and revised body contours, the P4 was tremendously fast and stable. All Daytona records were broken as four drivers hammered the P4 spider around for 580 test laps in the course of which the car was said to have touched 210mph. When the time for the race came in February 1967, this spider was backed by a completely new Berlinetta and sundry older cars, and as the flying Chaparral crashed and Ford after Ford went out with transmission failure, the Ferraris sailed on virtually untroubled, their engine compartments never even opened, until they lined up three abreast for the last three laps, to stage a mass finish that made the Ford performance at Le Mans the previous year look amateurish. It was a stunning victory, and one that Ferrari never let anybody forget.

Perhaps this was because they had little subsequent success to shout about. At Le Mans the P4s had performed well and were driven in a steady and level headed manner while letting most of the opposition blow itself up; but one of

Above: On show at Turin in 1963, the car that should have followed the 250 GTO into production: the rear-engined Type 250LM. Below: 250LM engine bay. Right: Surtees brings the P3 Ferrari prototype into the pits during the 1966 Nurburgring 1,000km race, as damper troubles begin to slow the car after a tremendously fast start. The right rear tyre eventually wore through the bodywork

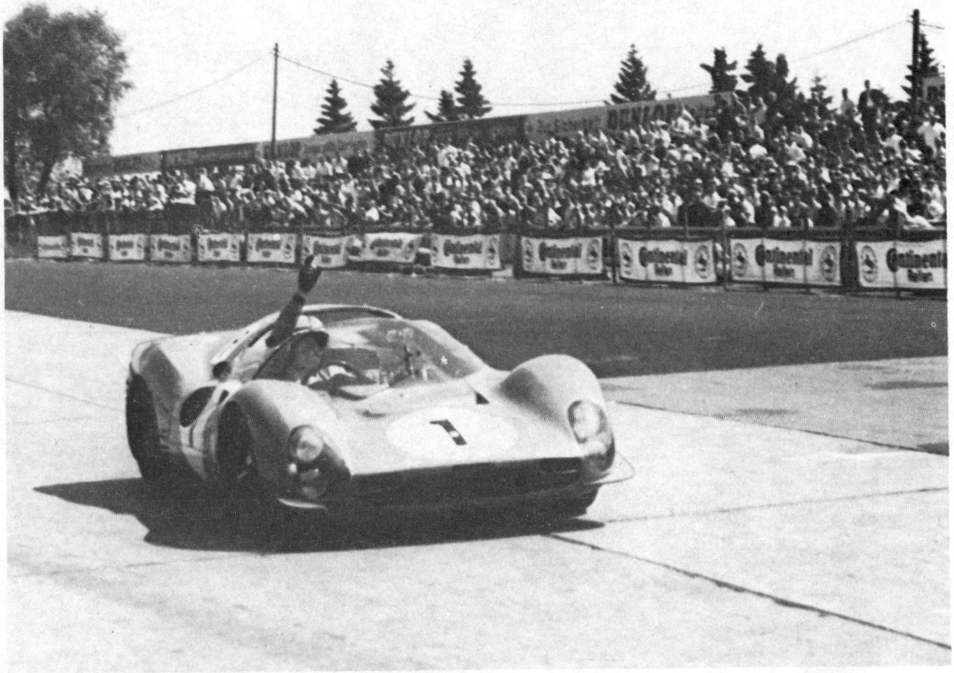
Continental

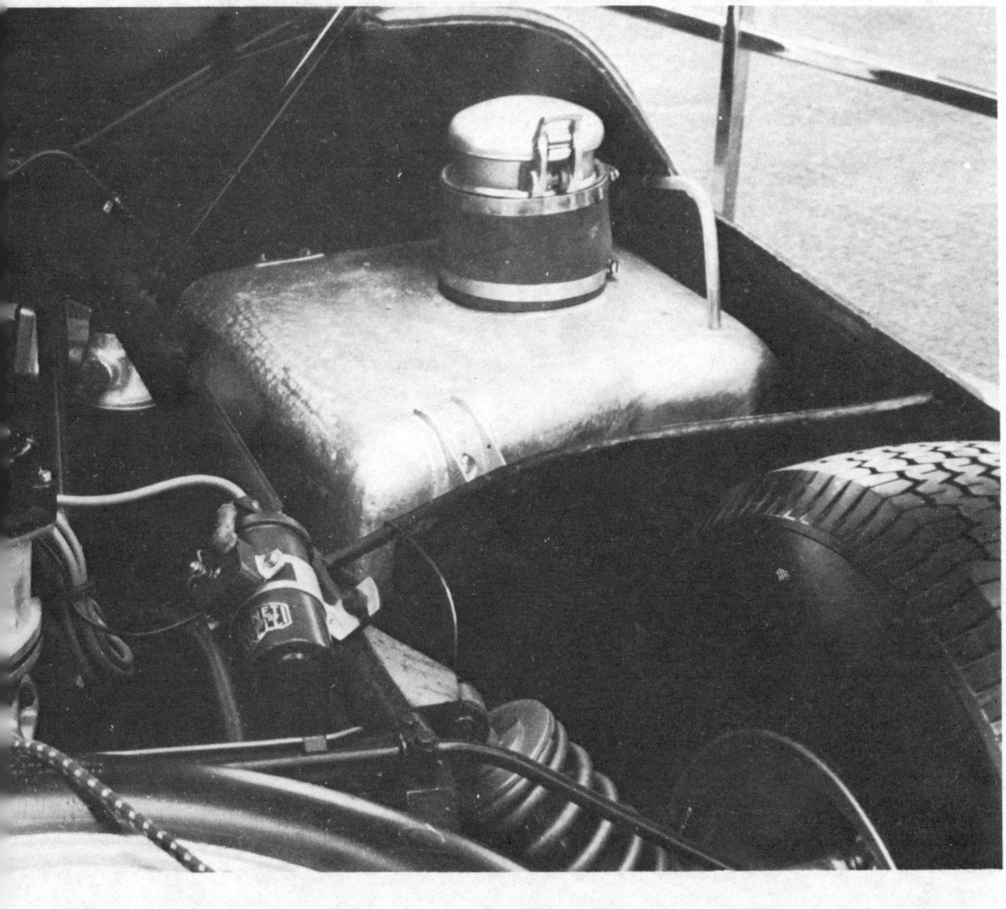

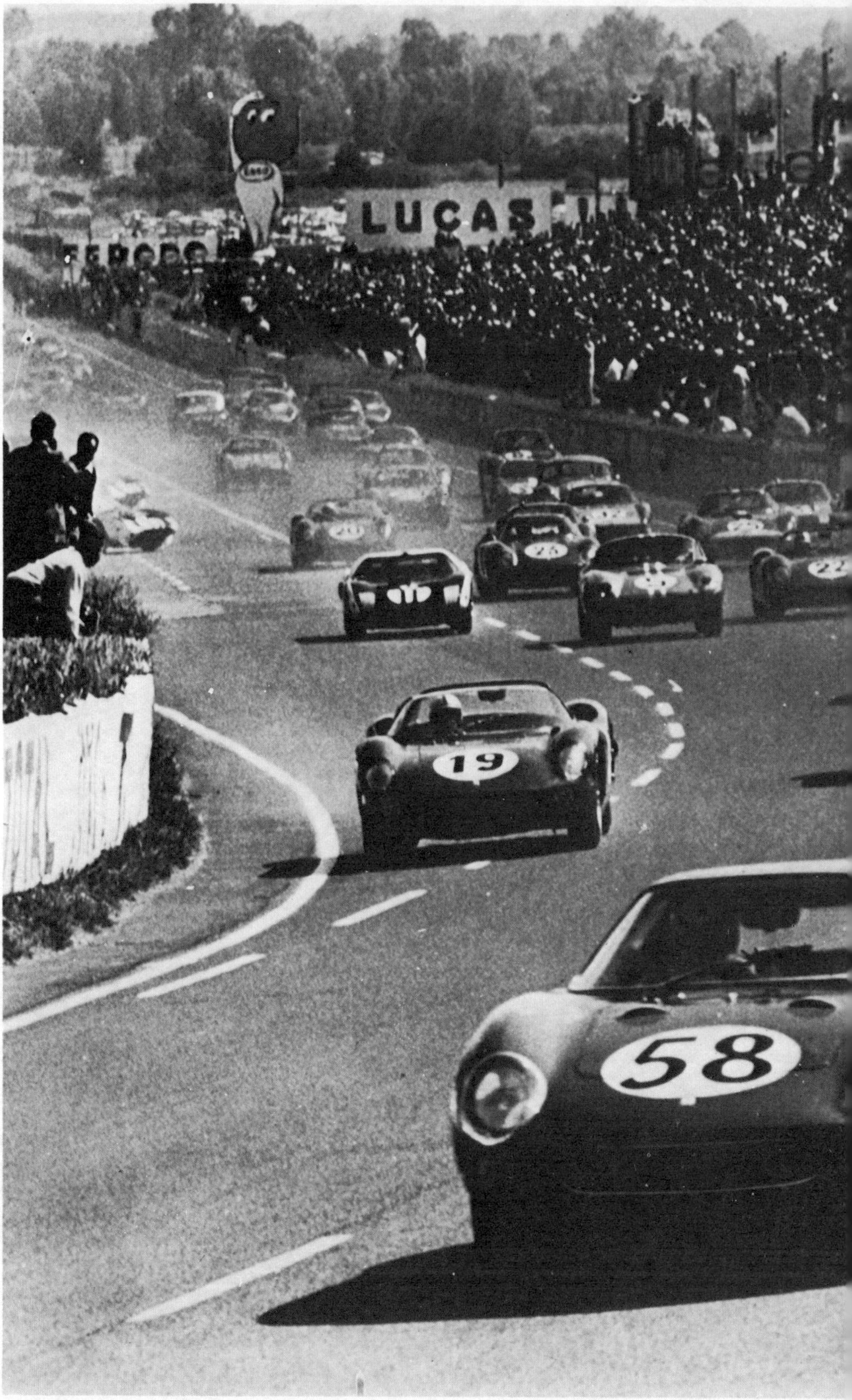
LUCAS
19
58

Le Mans 1964, with Piper's 250LM (actually a 3.3-litre or Type 275) leading Salmon's Aston Martin and the rest of the horde at the start

The little 2-litre Dino was often surprisingly fast in bigger-engine company, as was this one, driven by van Rooyen and Dean in South African events in 1968

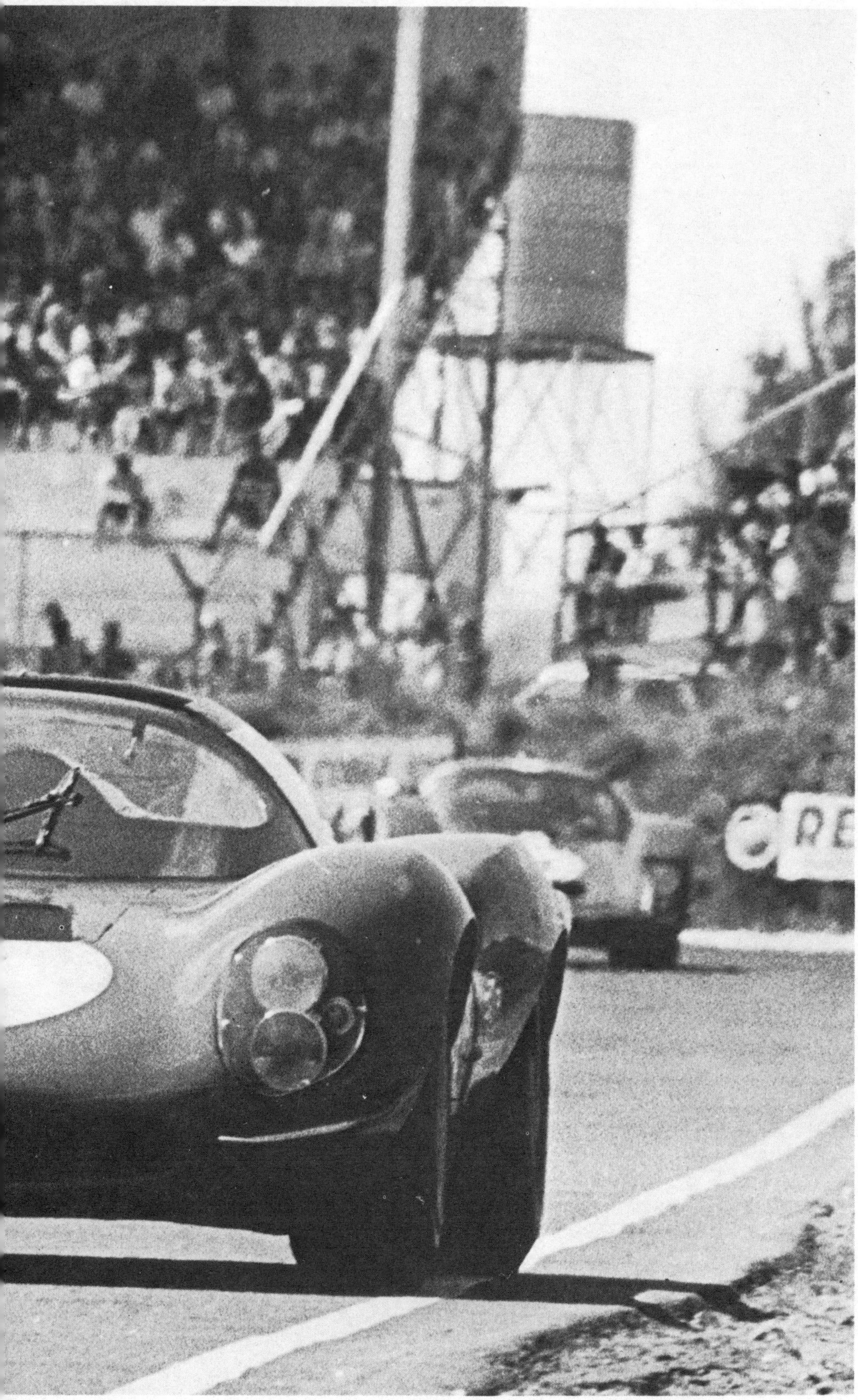

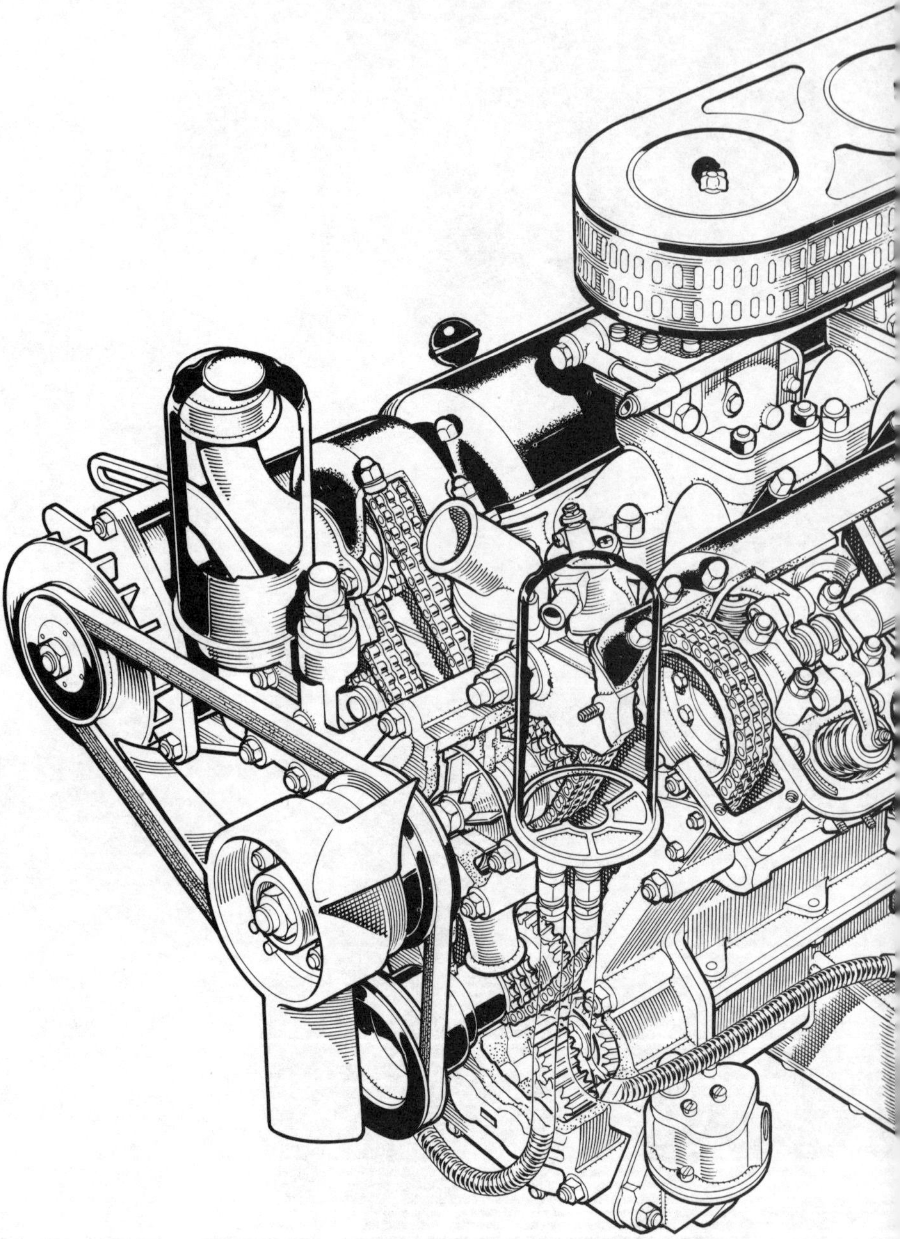

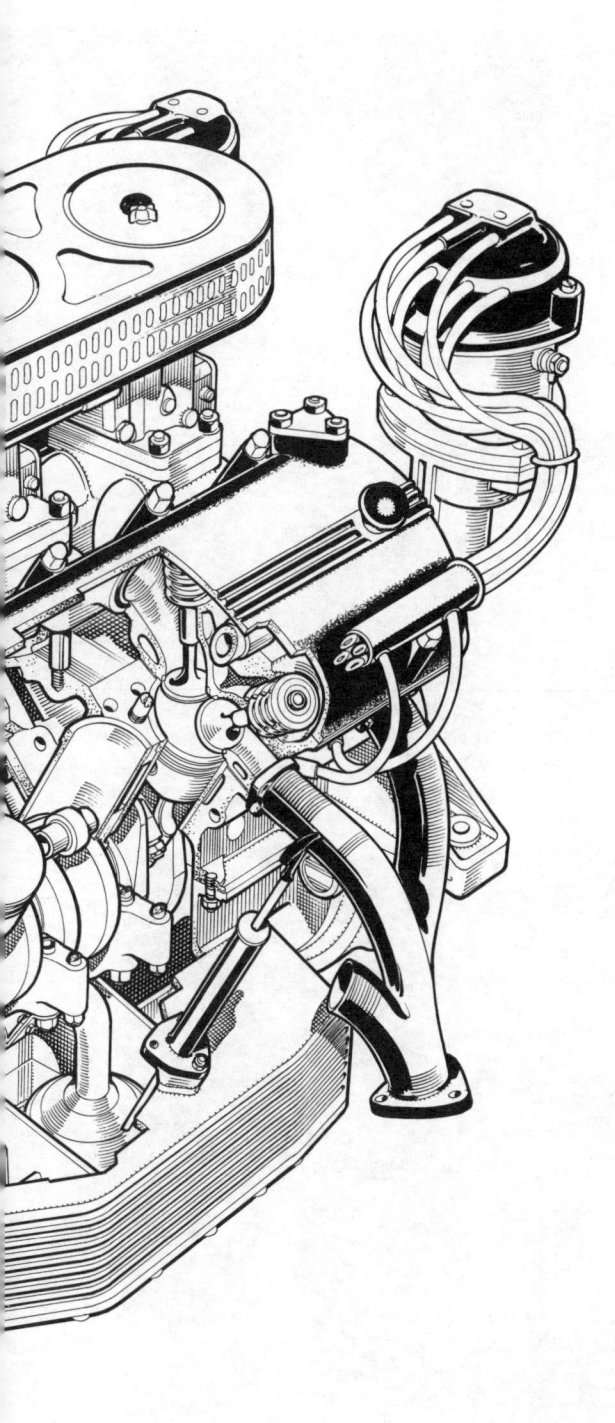

1964 250 GT Ferrari V 12 Engine

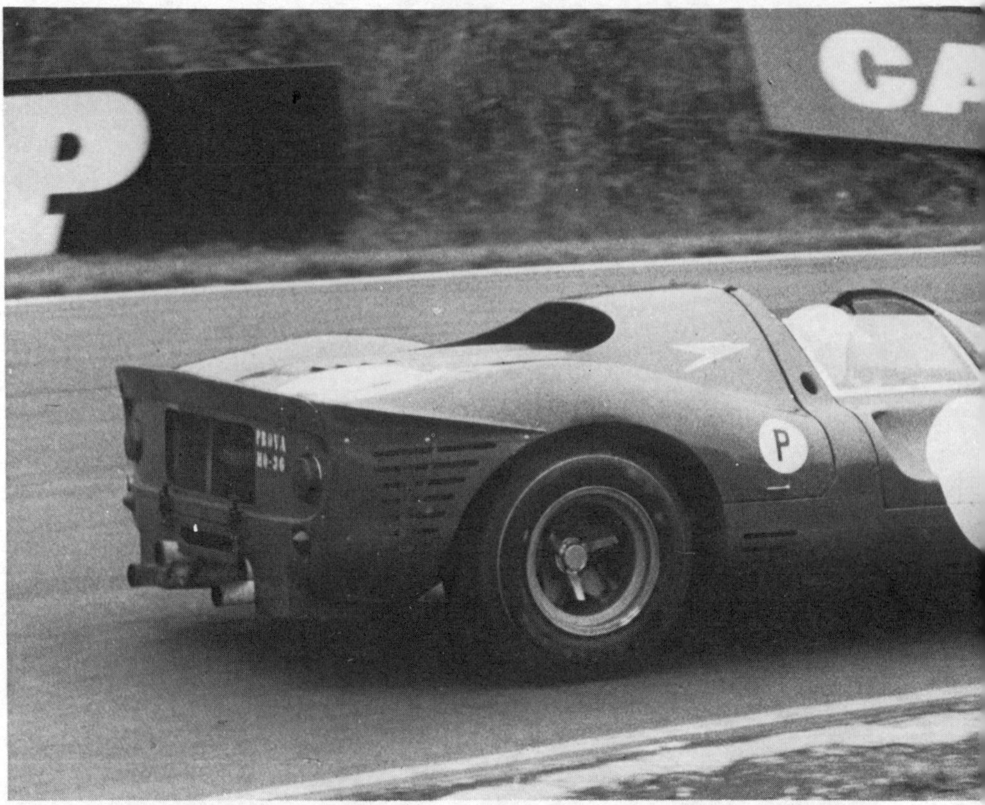
P

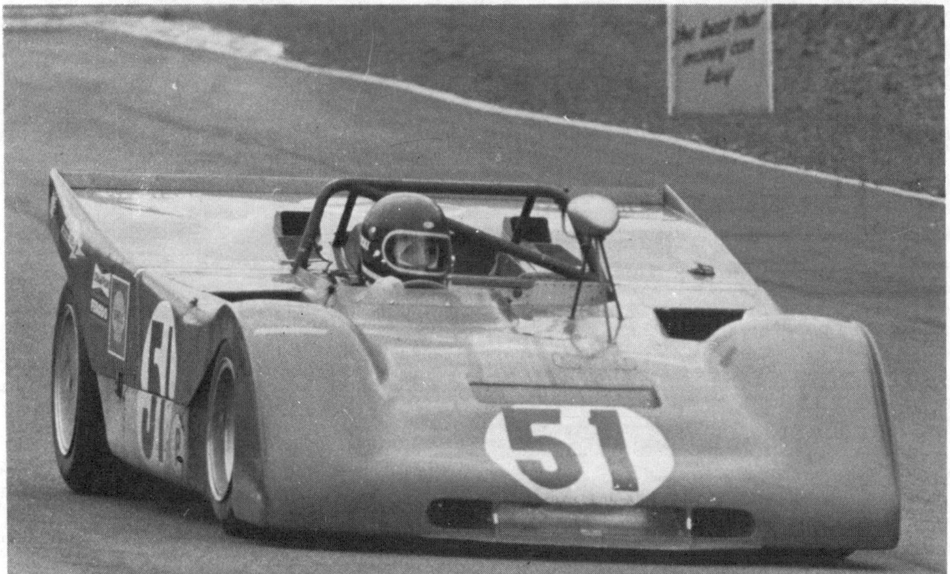
51

Winning the sports car championship of 1967 while finishing second to a Chaparral in the Brands Hatch 1,000km race, the 450 bhp P4 at the top of Druids Hill hairpin

the Fords was allowed to get too far ahead, and though the second place P4 narrowed the gap at a tremendous rate in the closing hours, it could never quite catch up. Moreover Porsche had been achieving some success in other sports car events, so that the points standings for the manufacturers' championship were extremely close after Le Mans and everything turned on the results of the Brands Hatch race. This turned out to be an immensely exciting event, for on the road it was a race between the Ferraris and the lone Chaparral, while on paper it was between Ferrari and Porsche. The Chaparral was a convincing winner, while Ferrari beat Porsche by the time it took the latter to change a set of brake pads, and thus became champion manufacturer yet again, for the tenth time in the fifteen-year history of the championship. In the following year Ferrari would not be competing, for the regulations had been changed yet again to limit the engines of sports-racing prototypes to 3-litres while permitting the group 4 cars (those which had been produced in a greater quantity) engines of 5-litres capacity. Ferrari, having on his hands ten superb and very expensive 4-litre engines that were thus at a stroke rendered useless, promptly went into a furious retirement from sports car racing.

If no publicity is worse than bad publicity, it may be that he did the wrong thing. In the absence of the red Italians, the Americans and Germans virtually took over sports car racing and all the classics were fought out by Ford and Porsche. Inevitably the pattern was repeated in 1969, when Ferrari took a little interest and sent some new 3-litre V12 engined spiders to a few of the early races. These type 312P cars were certainly fast, frequently leading or putting up fastest lap, but they were usually slowed by some misfortune and never won anything. Frequently only one was entered against several cars from the German and American factories who had no other important racing commitments to satisfy, no teams of Formula 1 cars to support and maintain. Likewise it is difficult to detect any great enthusiasm on the part of the Ferrari factory for the cars which they sent across the Atlantic to take part in the CanAm series of races, although their big Rocchi V12s may form the basis of interesting future developments, as may the flat-12 Forghieri engine of the all-conquering Ferrari GP car of 1970. After all, a Ferrari sports car is really a Ferrari racing car, *mutatis mutandis*.

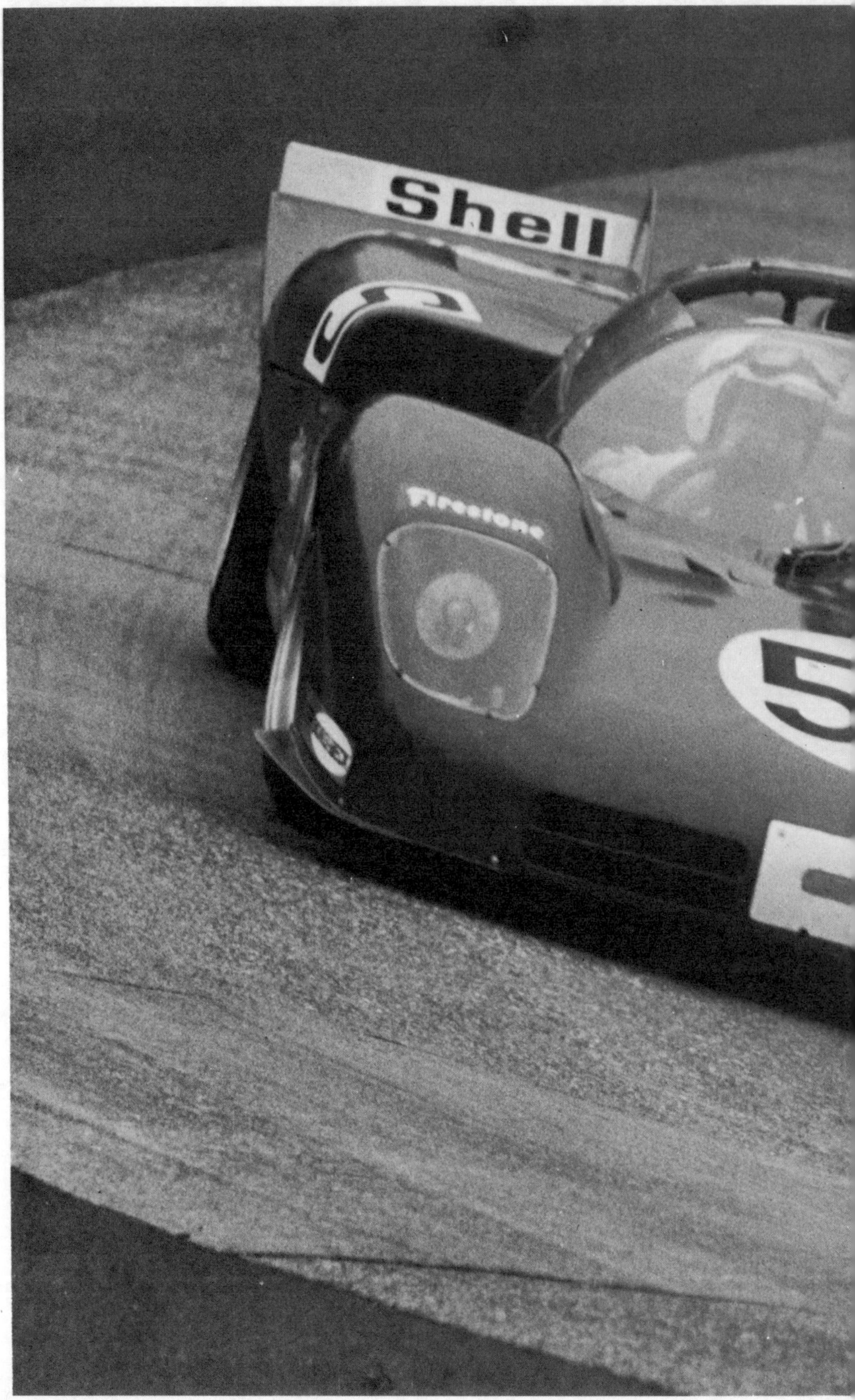
Shell
Firestone
5

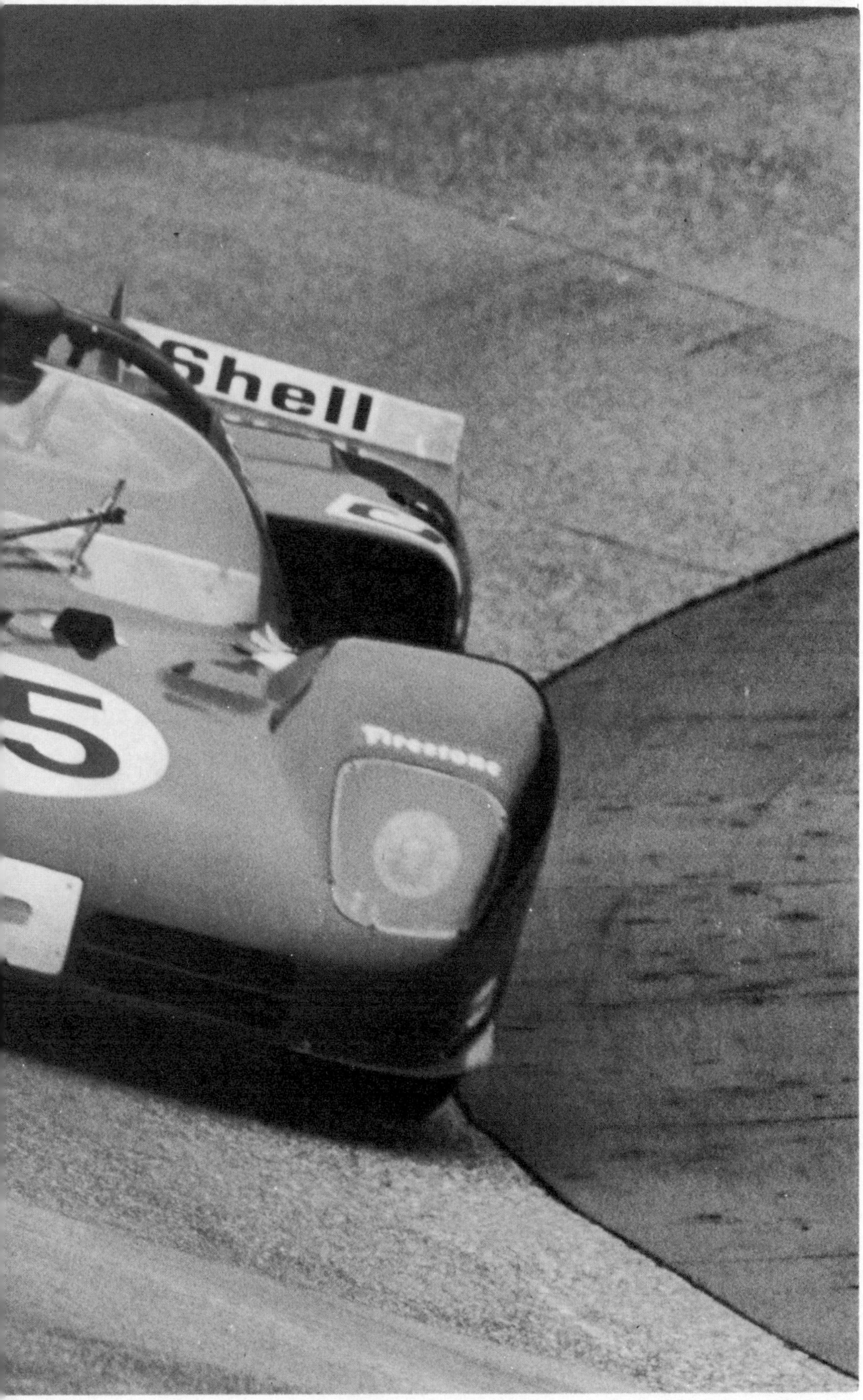
Shell

FERRARIS IN THE STREET

In 1947 the Ferrari factory produced three cars. In 1970 the output ran into four figures. Of the intervening period the first half may be dismissed as one in which Ferrari was struggling to grow, fighting to build a reputation on the racing circuits of the world, until in or about 1955 he realised that there was now money and a reputation to be made out of building touring cars in quantity, and that he had available a design that lent itself to the project. Prior to that he had not committed himself much to the manufacture of touring cars, just building the occasional example now and then for the odd customer, so that in his first ten years he had produced no more than 600 cars. Of these, several were built in series of no more than five, and even then they might differ appreciably from one example to another. There were therefore plenty of different models and innumerable variations upon them, the complexity of the output being heightened by the fact that bodies for these cars were built by all manner of coach builders, the majority of them more memorable for their enthusiastic vulgarity than for anything else. Nevertheless some attractive designs were produced, especially in the early days when the basic characteristics of the Ferrari production car were established as a sort of expansive variation on the Cisitalia theme.

The first touring car from the Ferrari factory was the type 166 Inter. This was a detuned long-wheelbase version of the two-litre Mille Miglia car and its specification included a number of oddities, the most peculiar being a five-speed gearbox in which third and fourth speeds were graced with synchromesh, and a most troublesome rigid rear axle with its light alloy centre casting for the differential assembly. This axle was to be one of the weak spots of the transmission, as was the clutch. As described in another chapter, many of these and other such components in the early cars were adapted from mass-production designs (usually from low-powered Fiats) and it was asking a lot that they should cope with the elevated power output of the V12 Ferrari engine.

For all that, the 166 Inter was a most appealing car; and it was soon given the appeal of more torque and power by being increased in capacity to 2.56-litres. This was the 212 Inter, and when produced as a shorter-wheelbased version it was known as the 212 Export. These distinctions were retained by Ferrari for the next models, which had grown to a full 3-litres: these were the type 250, and were based on the big Lampredi V12 rather than the little Colombo design. Indeed, from 1950 onwards the story gets increasingly comlicated with two different series of V12 engines being moved in and out of any chassis that were available in the factory, or so it seems.

It is probably unfair to Lampredi to consider his engines as being merely a development of Colombo's. Since he was in effect being invited to make a fresh start by producing a $4\frac{1}{2}$-litre unsupercharged V12 that would be competitive in Grand Prix racing, it is clear that he had little cause to adopt any of the features of the little $1\frac{1}{2}$-litre engine with which Colombo had set Ferrari on his way, save the basic V12 configuration. In fact the differences beyond this were very considerable. It was not just a question of the block being four inches longer, because of the increased distances between bore centres. A growth in conrod width by 1 millimetre was equally irrelevant. Undoubtedly the most important feature of the Lampredi design was his use of screwed-in wet cylinder liners eliminating the fire joint and leaving only o-rings at the base to seal the water and oil. Thus the cylinder head and block became one unit which could be bolted to the crankcase, whereas Colombo had a more conventional block designed with shrunk wet cylinder liners and detachable heads relying upon a gasket to ensure that fire and water did not

For a climate even finer than Italy's there was this 250GT Spyder named the California

mix. In the matter of valve gear there was something to be said for each version: Colombo started by using finger cam followers or lever tappets, but Lampredi used rollers for his cam followers and all the later Colombo engines did likewise. Again Lampredi was more thoroughgoing in his attention to porting: all his engines had twelve separate intake ports, whereas many of Colombo's engines had only six. A particularly nasty feature of Colombo's early designs was the extreme angle at which the connecting rods were split across the big ends, a bad practice which has nothing to commend it save that it provides for the withdrawal of the connecting rods through the cylinder bores. Lampredi would have none of this, and the perpendicular split of his big ends is conducive to much greater strength and better distribution of inertia loads on the bearing surfaces. On the other hand Lampredi's engines were more impractical in various ways, more difficult to work on, and more susceptible to trouble in the plumbing both of oil and of water.

The first car to go on the road with the Lampredi 'long' V12 was the type 340 America announced in 1950. The car weighed less than a ton and had 220 bhp to push it, or so the factory brochure said; but power output claims were even less to be trusted in those days than they are now, though there is little reason to doubt the accompanying claim of a 137mph maximum speed. It was after all a sports car, but was followed in 1951 by a grand tourer, the 342 America upon which all subsequent big Ferraris were based. It had what it needed most of all, which was a heavier

While the competition Ferrari always looked functional and good, the early tourers seldom looked either. This Farina body, based on the original Type 250 Europa, needed several facelifts to become a passable 250GT

and sturdier centre section for the rear axle. The ratio within this was pretty high, too high in most of the bigger Ferraris in fact, so that although they were all capable of impractically high maximum speeds and were remarkably long legged in cruising, their acceleration was less dramatic than might have been expected. This did not help the car's reputation in the American market, where acceleration was the only aspect of performance that was really understood and the pleasures of using a gearbox were not generally to be appreciated for many years to come. Still, for those who wanted them the big Ferraris continued to be built, either as the 4.1-litre America, 4.5-litre Super America or the 4.9-litre Superfast. There were not many of them, since they were built at a rate not exceeding one a month.

It was the engine of the 4.1-litre

The 1949 Paris Show car ... little changed when the following year it was called a Le Mans coupe

139

America which, linered down to 3-litres, provided the engine for the original type 250 Export, the smallest version of the Lampredi long-block V12 ever made. The engine was not entirely a success and was subsequently replaced by a version of the earlier Colombo V12. Not that it really mattered a great deal, for at this stage what Ferrari really needed to learn was chassis design rather than engine perfection. Too often one reads in a press description some such expression as 'Trailing links with semi-elliptic leaf springs took care of the rear suspension' when patently they did nothing of the sort. Inadequate control of the rear axle was as much to blame as the generous power of the engines for the wheel-spinning proclivities of many Ferrari production cars, to the detriment of performance and handling.

It was in the 410 Superfast, a lightweight car with shortened wheelbase and not much more than a ton for its 4.9-litre engine to push around, that a de Dion rear suspension was adopted in a touring Ferrari. Even then the factory could not get away from their confounded leaf springs, and it was years before the touring cars' dampers, steering boxes and drum brakes ceased to betray the venerable age of the basic concept. Of course the body builders did their best to put a pretty new face forward on Ferrari's behalf, and in some cases they were quite successful, especially Touring of Milan in the very early days, later Michelotti, Vignale and ultimately Pininfarina with the 250 Europa.

It was the 250 Europa that set Ferrari on his way to becoming a production engineer as well as a specialist. Once he realised that he could adopt assembly-line procedures and avoid maintenance and spares problems that always hitherto discouraged him from producing more than ten or so of any given model, he dropped the Europa connotation from the 250 Europa GT and in 1957 went into production with a series of Pininfarina and Scaglietti bodies which somehow caught the imagination of the motoring press and

Many different styles were tried on the Type 410 Super America chassis. This 1959 two-seater coupe is by Pininfarina

of more members of the public than could actually afford to buy the car. From this point Ferrari never looked back, except to consider the history of the big Lampredi-engined cars and reduce the number that might be built in the future.

Lampredi having in any case departed some time earlier, there was no reason for the factory to rely on the compact little Colombo V12. This engine in the 250GT chassis made the touring Ferrari what it is today, something very different from the 250GT, the first of the assembly-line Ferraris, but nevertheless something that would not have been brought into existence without it.

Undoubtedly it was the two-seater grand-tourer coupés that made the 250 GT famous, the Berlinettas whose styling came from the 375 Mille Miglia

Ghia in 1961 did this to a Super America, evidently taking the name to heart

cars. They were classical roadgoing cars, but it was feasible to use them in racing of the right sort, and many an enthusiastic amateur driver did so with gratifying results. Once the idea caught on, the sporting GT Berlinettas rapidly got better and better, with Scaglietti producing the definitive short-wheelbase version which became famous in 1959, 1960 and 1961. In many ways they made far more sense than the bigger and slower touring versions, which seemed to retain all their disadvantages without having any compensating virtues. Many potential customers had argued that if the touring 250 GTs were not to be as rabidly fast as the SWB (short wheelbase Berlinetta)

The Superfast eventually became the sharp ended high-geared 2-seater seen here, a Pininfarina-bodied 400SA

versions they ought at least to be more capacious; and as a concession to them the first true four-seater Ferrari was produced in 1960. This was the 250GT 2+2, alias the GTE, and it was only a four-seater in the sense that the two people in the rear might at best be small or at worst be what Pomeroy once described as bicrural amputees. The car was shown off in use as a course marshal's transport at Le Mans, and it caught on in a big way.

People seemed to like the Pininfarina body, seemed to dote on the idea of having a Ferrari in which the whole family could travel, and seemed to be protected from any awareness of the incompatability of the gearbox and its overdrive. By the standards of its time, perhaps it was not the gross over-

This 1956 Pininfarina effort on a 410SA became the first Ferrari Superfast

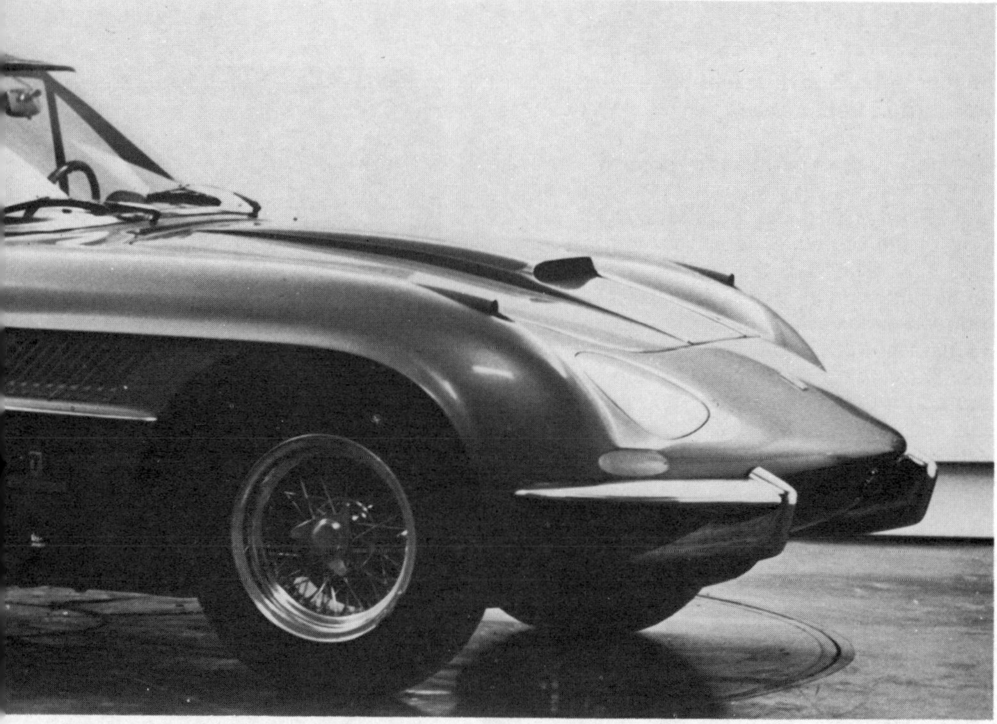

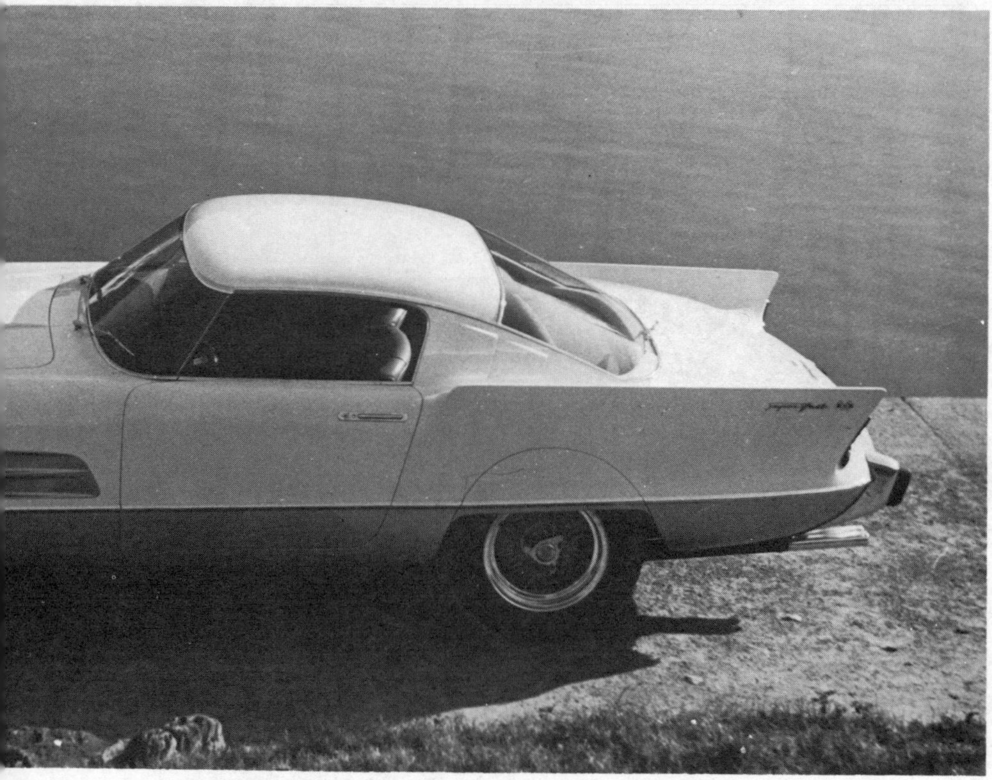

The functional short-wheel-base competition Berlinetta

decorated and tinny-looking contraption that it appears now, but at least it allowed Ferrari to extend the 250GT range in the opposite direction with a brace of Berlinettas that were more beautiful than anything that he had ever produced before, beautiful enough to rate just as highly today as they did in 1962. These were the 250GTO, the O standing for Omologato (or so it is said) and signifying that this was a car that could be used by the serious amateur racing driver; and the GT Berlinetta Lusso, which was as clearly specialised for high-speeds long-distance travel on public roads for two people and their necessary impedimenta. The Lusso was in fact the quintessence of the grand touring car as the idea had come to be understood, perfectly tractable, eminently rapid, and satisfying in its handling, braking, gearing and ride.

Since that significant year, the standard of production Ferraris has risen continually, for reasons that have been explained in an earlier chapter. In 1964 a new 4-litre version of the engine came along, and everybody who was not appalled by the four-headlamp styling of this new 330GT 2+2 acclaimed its new standards of smoothness and flexibility. Similarly, those who were not bewitched by its sheer performance and considerable roadholding were horrified by the lack of refinement in the body and of handiness in the steering. At least the 330 series was complemented by some new variations on the Berlinetta/GTO theme, with a 3.3-litre engine sitting at the nose, a five-speed gearbox-cum-final-drive in the tail, and wishbone independent suspension at all four corners. The 275 GTB and GTS (Berlinetta and Spider) were probably the most important things in the Ferrari production pro-

Quad headlamps on the 330GT were not well received, however well they worked

Above: Based on a 250GT chassis, this drophead has a strong family resemblance to King Leopold's America shown on an earlier page. Below: While the 275 and 330 series remained current, the 4.4-litre 365 was introduced as the California drophead in 1966. Right: Late in 1964 the 275 series appeared with 3.3-litre engine and independent rear suspension. This short-wheelbase open car was the GTS

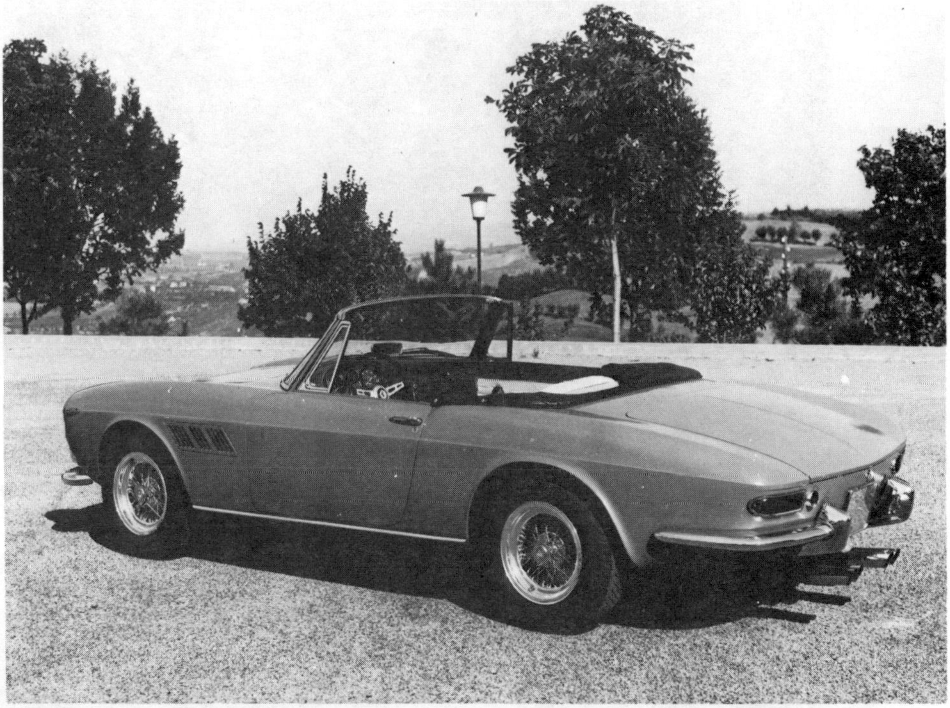

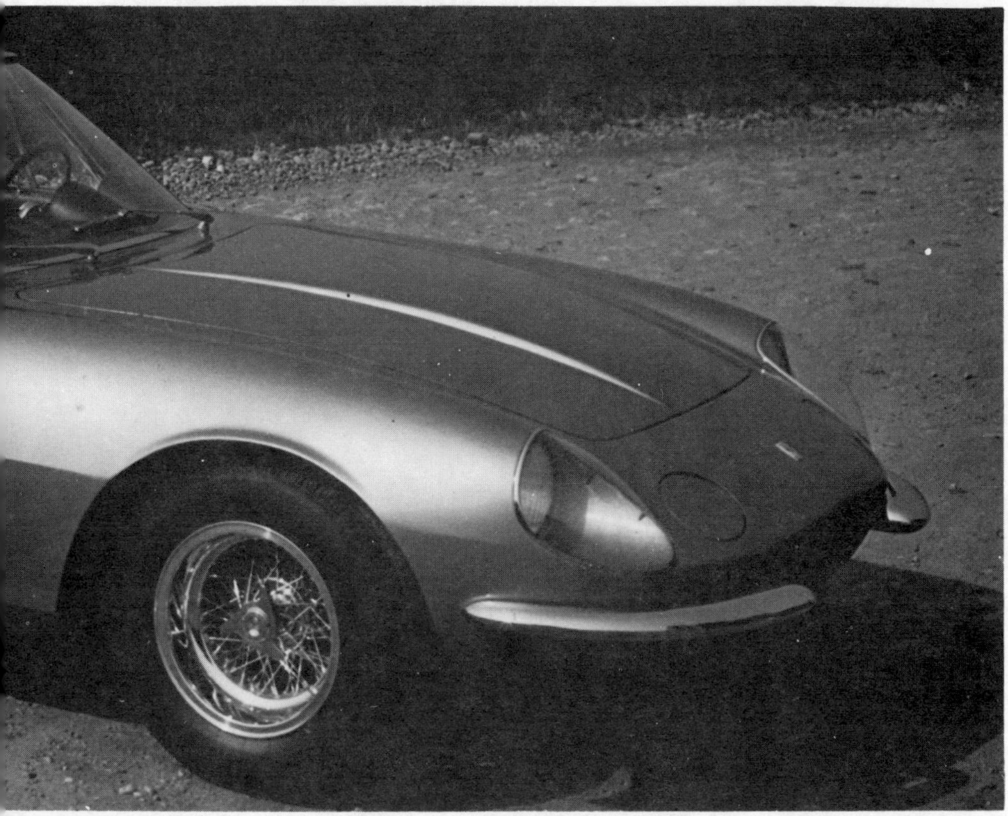

Closed version of the short 275 was this GTB, driven by the Author during some tyre trials at the Pirelli proving grounds. The 275GTB was popular among private owners wanting to do some racing in the GT category of long-distance classics

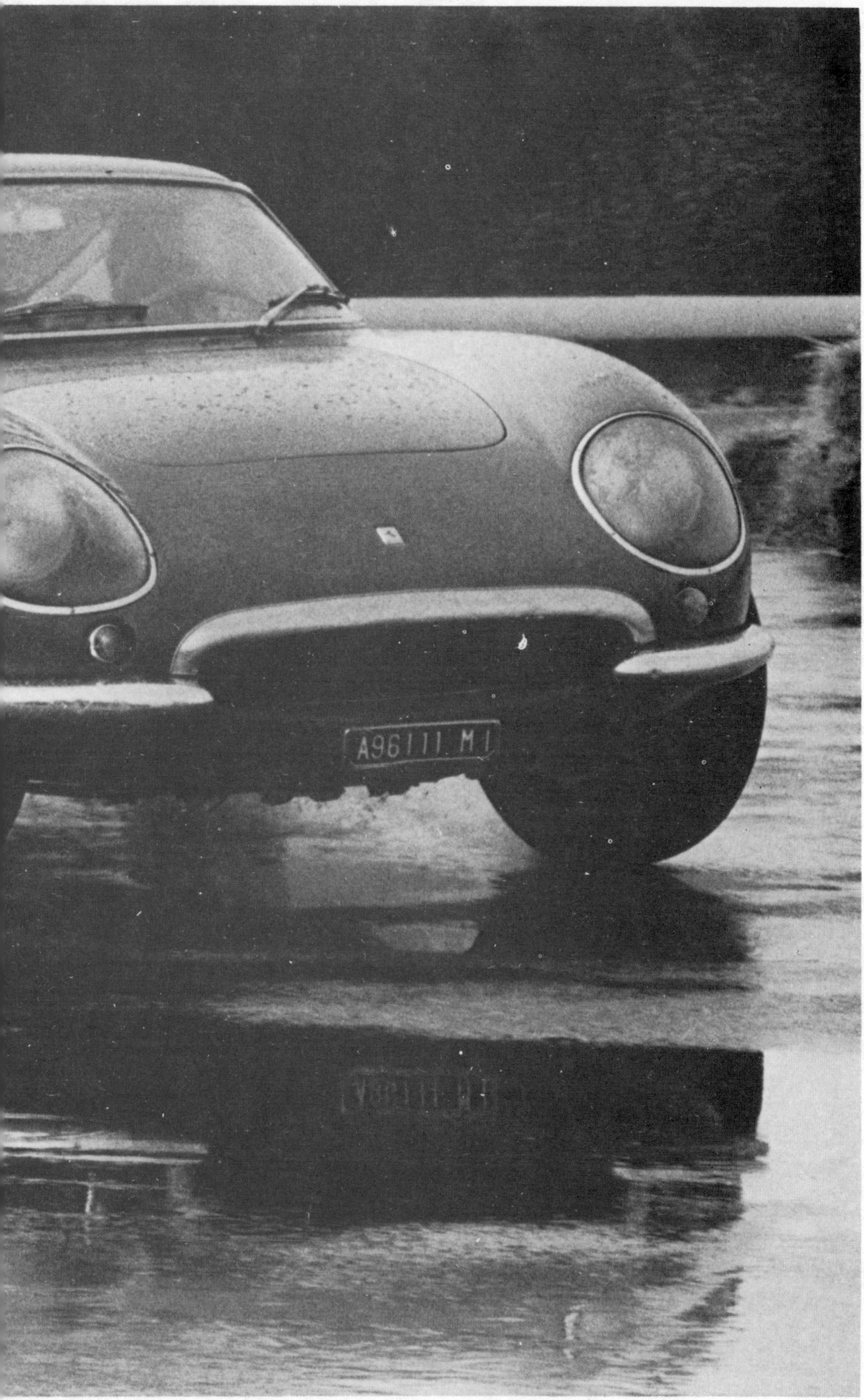
A96111 MI

Top: This singular car was specially built as a three-seater with central driving seat. Pininfarina showed it as Type 365P during 1966

Below: Nobody took this show-car seriously when it appeared in 1968. Christened the 250/P5, it had a rear-mounted 3-litre Grand Prix engine which some people said was not a wooden mock-up!

Below right: An altogether more practical rear-engined Ferrari to appear in 1968 was the beautiful little Farina-bodied Dino V6

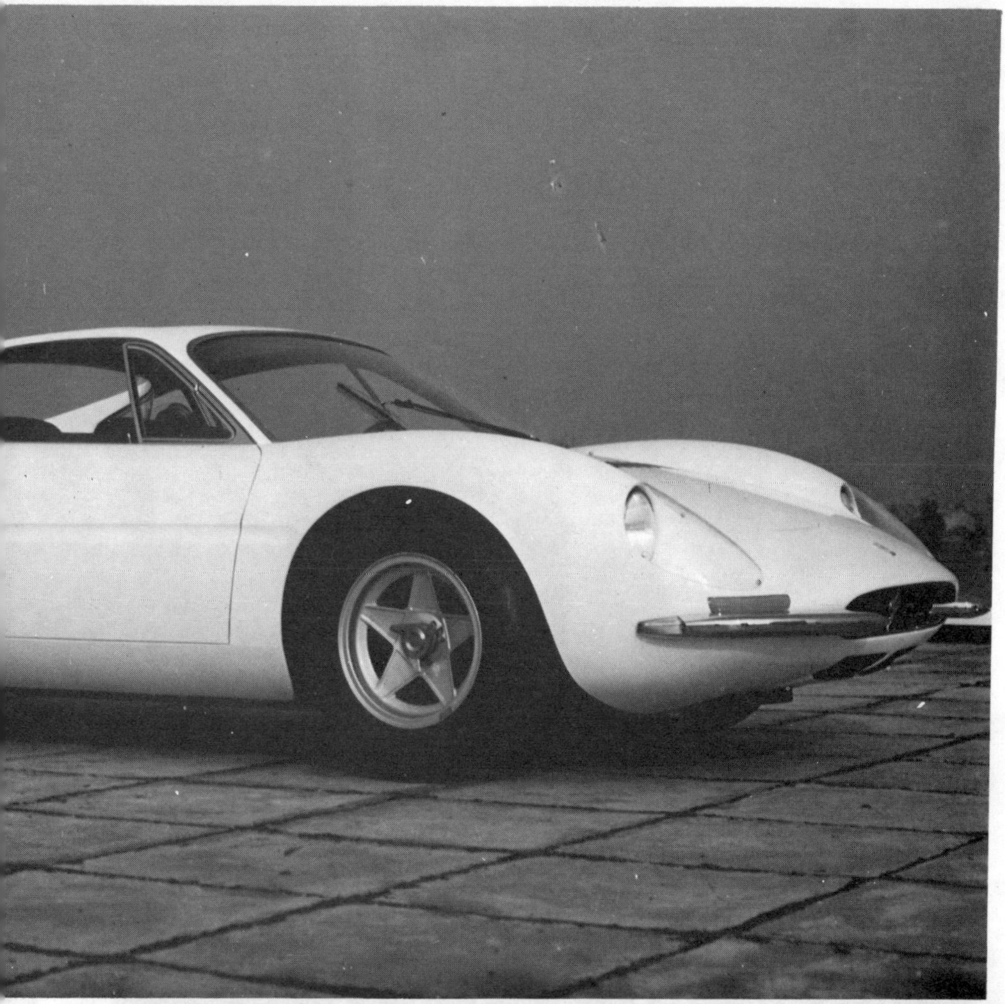

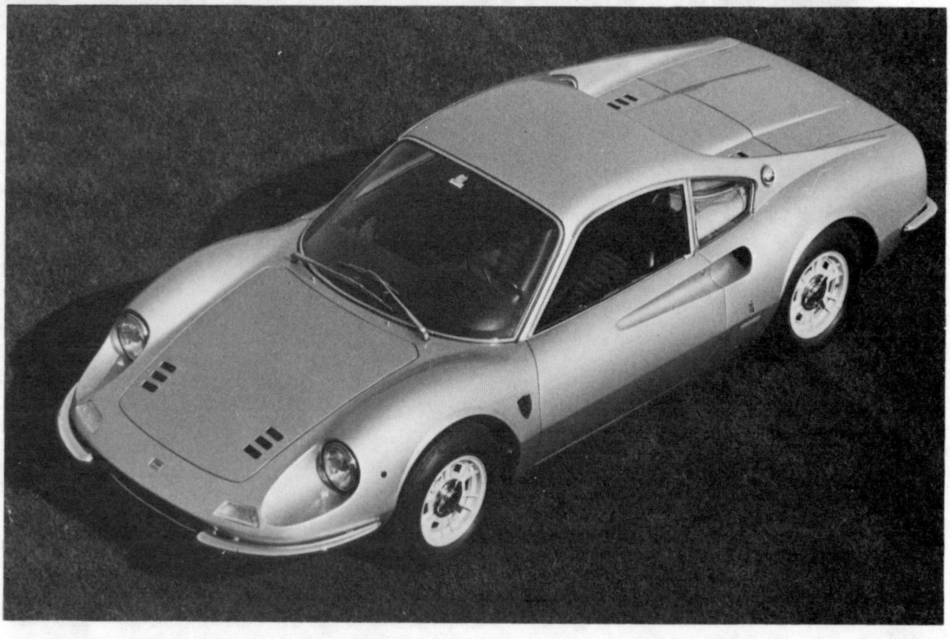

The special Berlinetta from which grew the Lusso

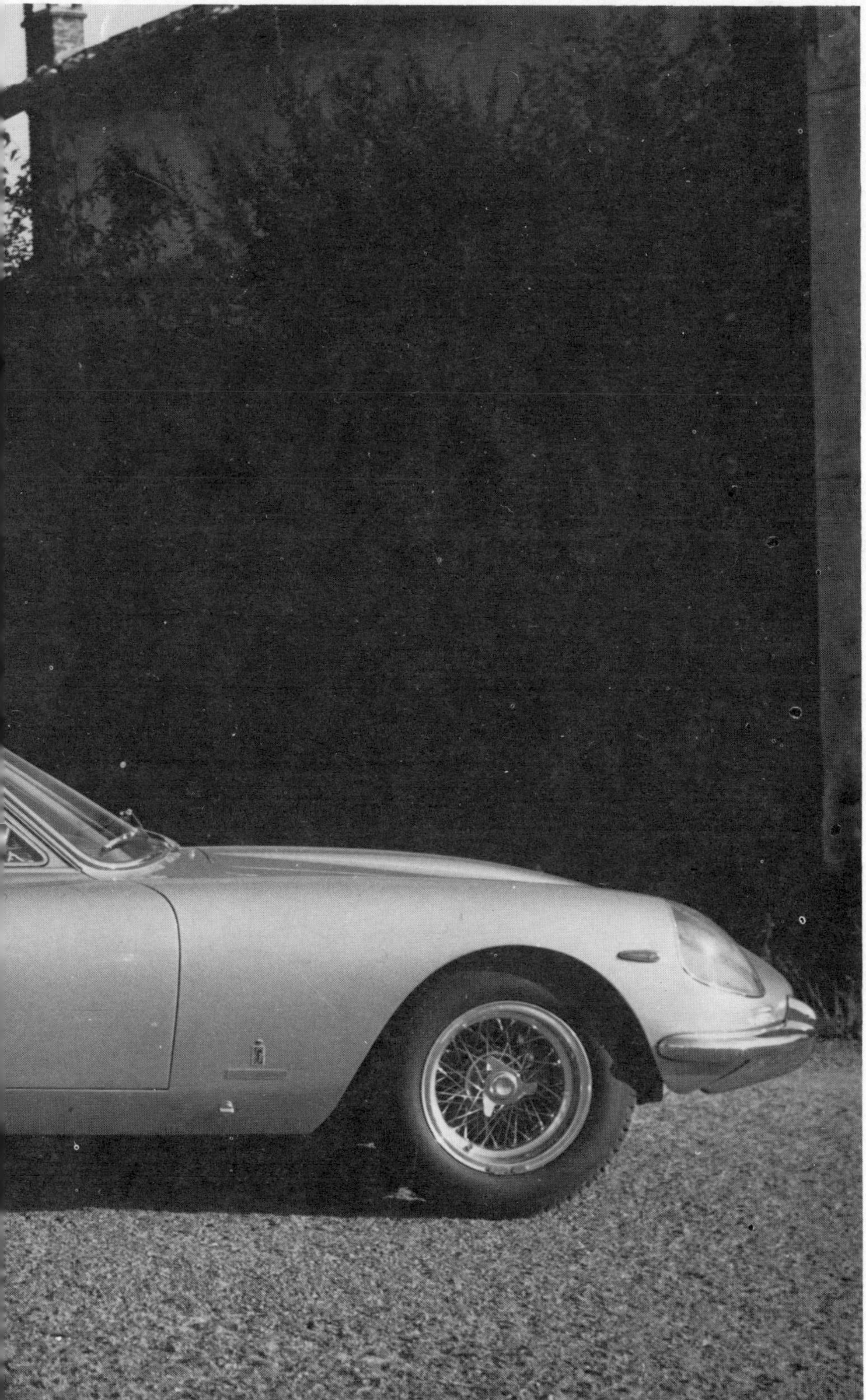

In 1967 the 365 range was expanded to include this rakish but very heavy GT 2+2

gramme since Lampredi went to work for Fiat; and when some minor problems were ironed out by encasing the propshaft in a torque tube Ferrari had an exceptional car. The four-cam version of the GTB was a real goer, and often did a lot to preserve Ferrari's reputation when other cars were losing theirs: but any 275GTB is a delight to drive, full of the spirit and response, and with steering and handling, roadholding and braking, of the highest class. This was a car in which the reserves of control and performance seemed almost limitless.

Only when the 365 series came along in 1968 after a preliminary year as the California convertible only, did these standards have to be revised. As a GT 2+2 the car was prodigious – roomy, quiet, smooth, level-riding at the rear (thanks to the use, for the first time in a production car, of the road-pumped self-levelling Koni damper strut) and compliant with the new American safety regulations. It weighed practically two tons laden, but with 320bhp to propel it the car was said to be capable of 152mph. It did not look nearly as exciting as those figures might imply but when you see one cruising along a European motorway at something like 130mph fully laden it undoubtedly looks impressive. Perhaps cars intended for such high-speed cruising

The lenticular nose of the 365 helps to fine down the car's lines, recalling the earlier GTO cars

should not look exciting: perhaps their quality should be taken for granted, not announced, as with a good London suit.

Except that it is only a two seater, the same applies to the 365GTC, which some commentators declared the best thing that Ferrari had ever built for sale to the public. When they made this declaration however they had not taken into account the dramatic new 365 GTB, the Daytona coupé, so named in honour of the gratifying occasion early in 1967 when three Ferraris finished in line abreast ahead of the rest of the field in the Daytona 24-hours sports-car race. This Berlinetta, with its extravagant new styling by Pininfarina and high standard of execution by Scaglietti, may have been conceived merely as an answer to the Lamborghini, which was now established as a rival of high quality and high performance. The Lamborghini Miura had taken a lot of the wind out of Ferrari's sails with its claimed maximum speed of 300 kilometres an hour, or 186mph, but the word gradually got around that the claim could not usually be substantiated, and that something over 170 mph was as much as could be relied on. To what extent this was true the author is not prepared to say, being conscious from his own experience that Lamborghinis vary a lot, since they are deliberately adjusted to suit the known techniques or shortcomings of individual customers. Nevertheless the Daytona Ferrari was put on the market with an uncompromising claim for 280km/h, or 174mph, and there seems no doubt of the accuracy of that figure. I personally have never driven it at more than 158mph, but the quality of the car, and the consistency of its handling at all speeds up to that, leave no doubts about the glory of Ferrari's accomplishment in evolving cars of impeccable performance, quality and breeding.

In 1968 appeared the fastest street Ferrari to go into production, the 365 GTB4 Daytona. Nose treatment is aerodynamically tidy but the plastics screening is very vulnerable Good penetration is as important as the four-cam engine in giving the 365GTB its claimed 174mph capability. In the author's limited experience of this model, the acceleration begins to tail off beyond 155mph

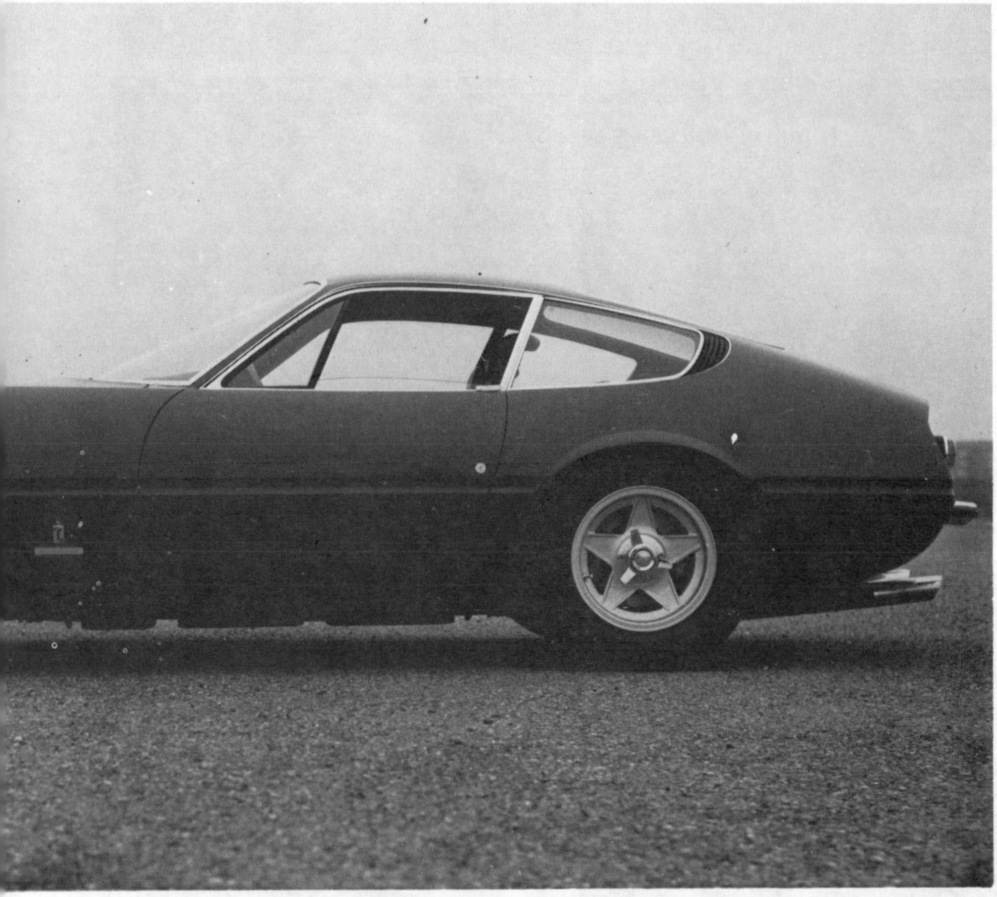

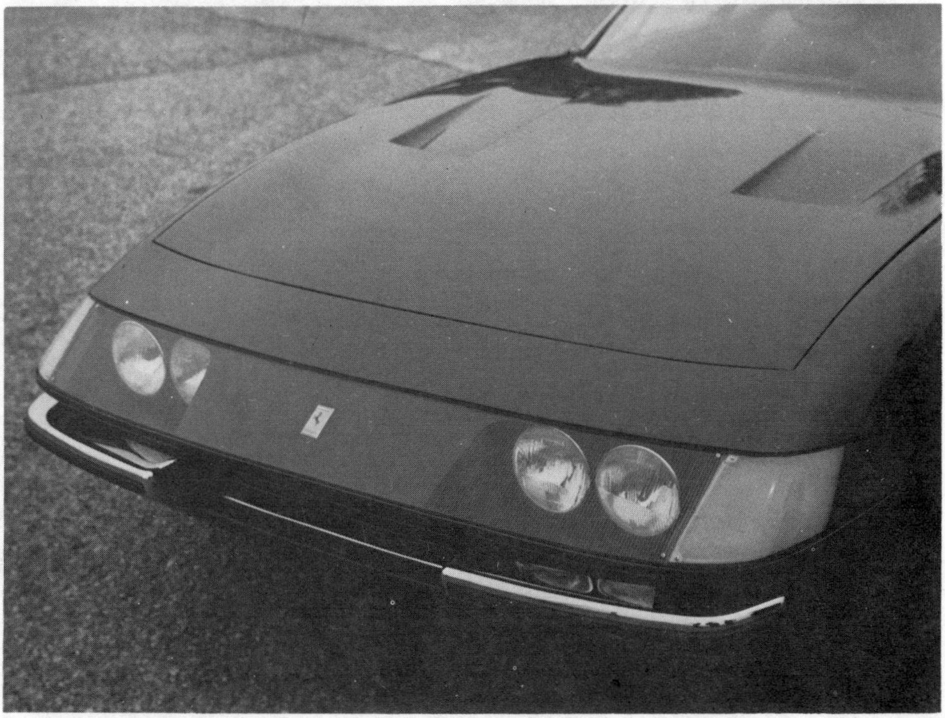

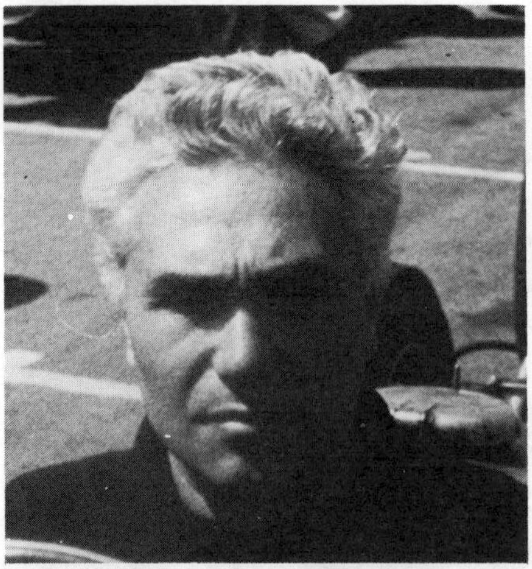
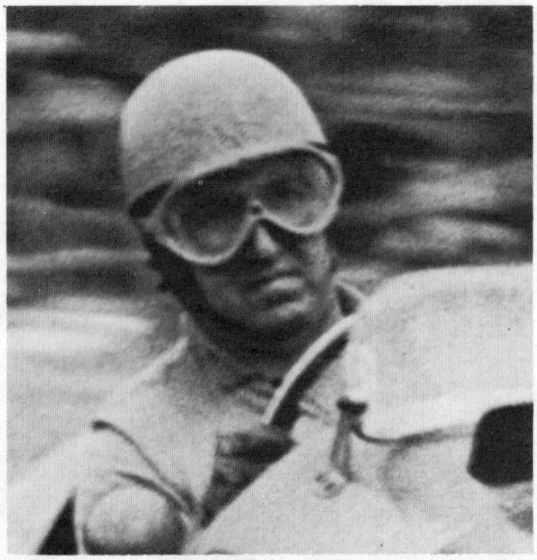
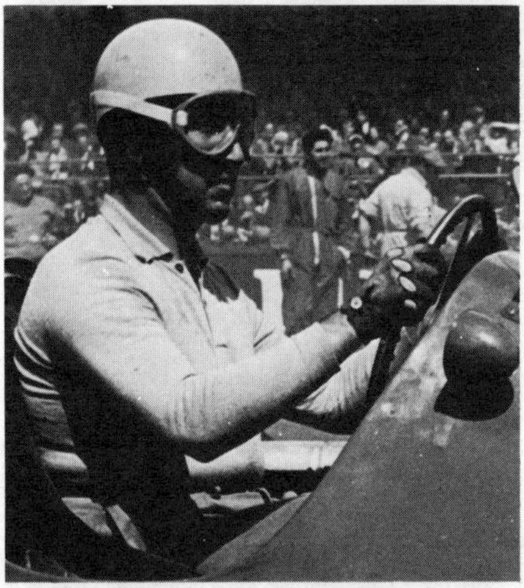
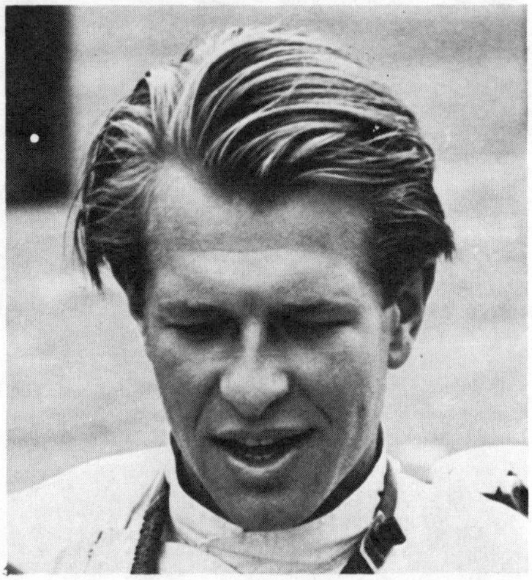
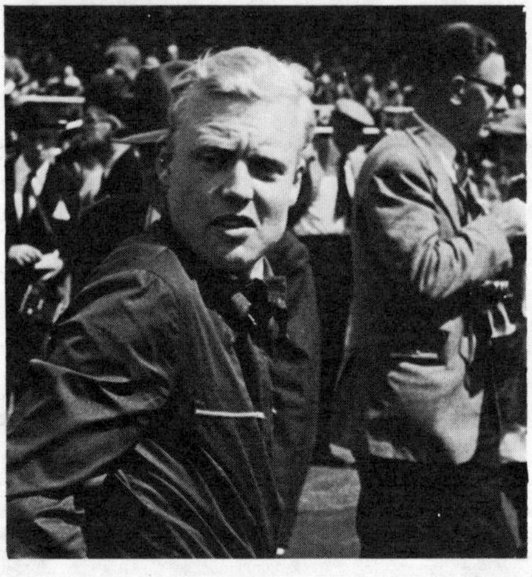
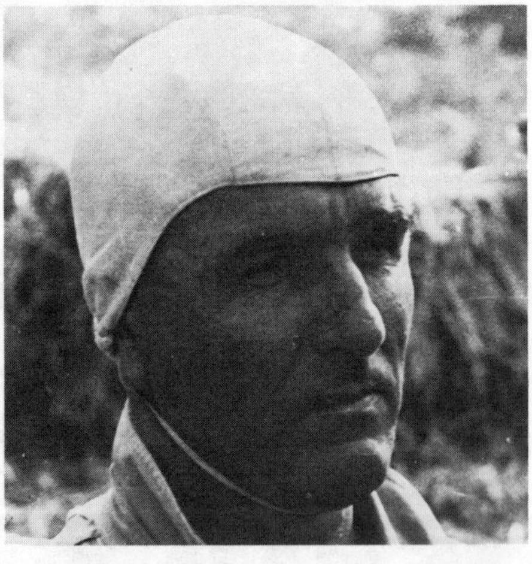

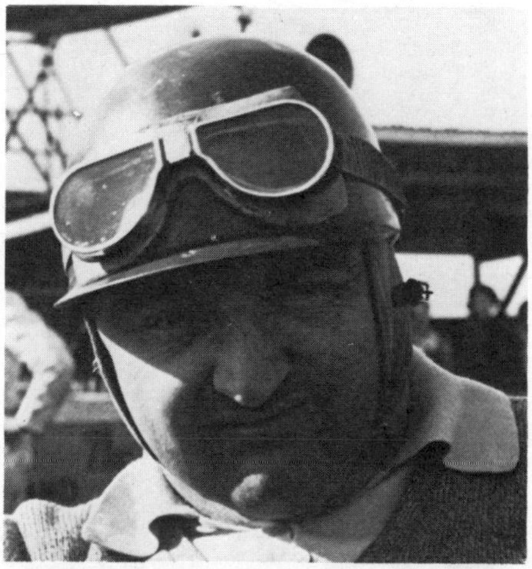
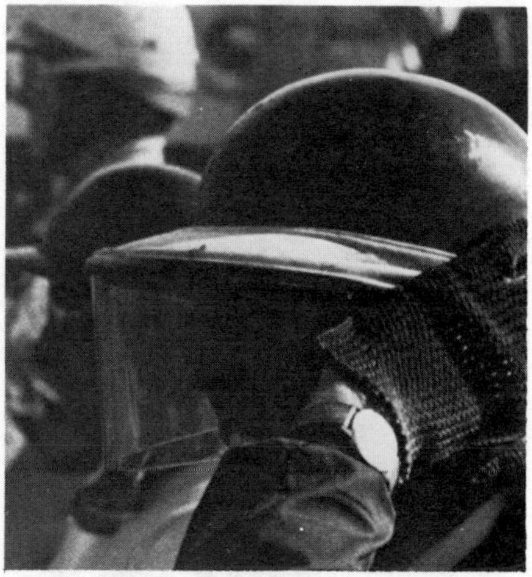
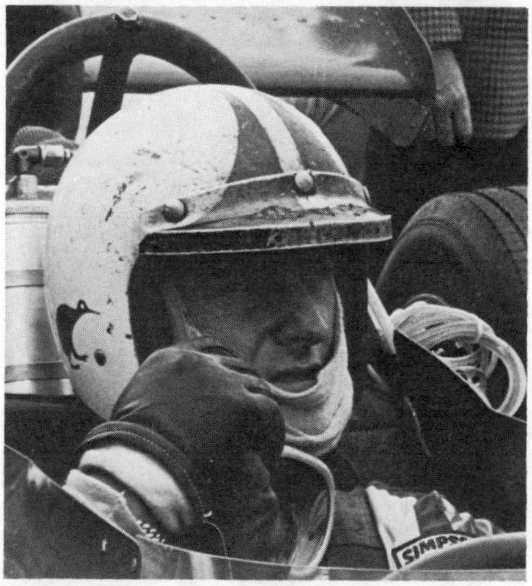
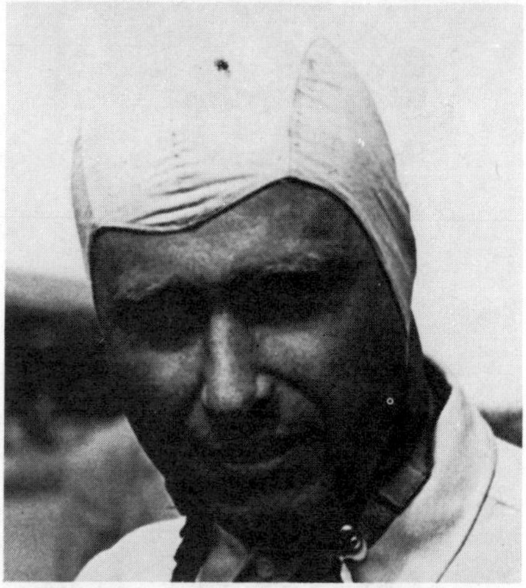
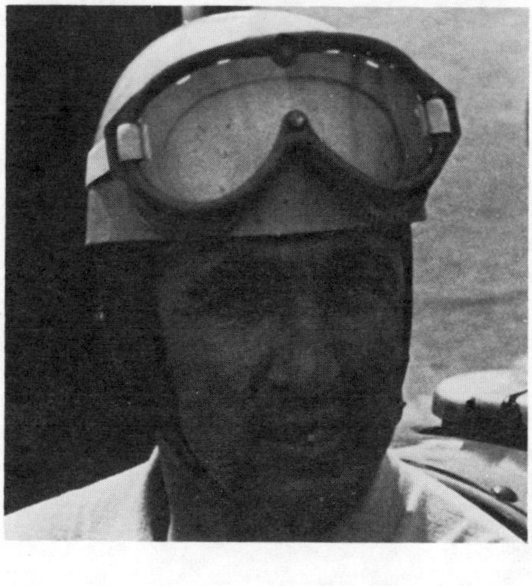
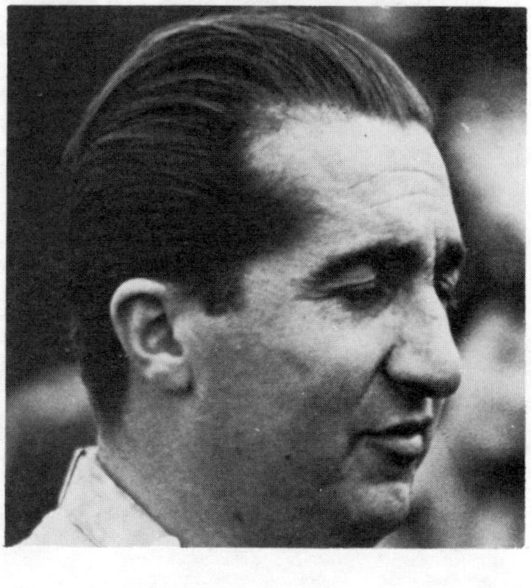

**The Author
L J K Setright**
With fifteen books on motoring, motorcycling, aviation and kindred subjects to his credit, L J K Setright is also a prolific contributor on these subjects to a surprising variety of magazines. He also does some work as an engineering consultant — an equally far cry from the lawyer's career upon which he originally embarked. With the distinction of having been invited to accept membership of both the Institution of Mechanical Engineers and the Institution of the Rubber Industry, LJKS insists that the remoteness of his subject matter from that of his fairly classical schooling is insignificant. Wide acclaim for his style confirms his theory that if language be not accorded priority over subject, then the subject can be given no reliable priority at all.

Film production Piagraph Limited
Ballantine Consultant Editor Prince Marshall
Foulis Production Editor Tim Parker